WOODWORKING

Step-by-step Guide to Learn the Best Techniques

(The Complete Guide to Help You Create Easy Woodworking Projects)

George Nicholas

Published By Bella Frost

George Nicholas

All Rights Reserved

Woodworking: Step-by-step Guide to Learn the Best Techniques (The Complete Guide to Help You Create Easy Woodworking Projects)

ISBN 978-1-77485-295-8

All rights reserved. No part of this guide may be reproduced in any form without permission in writing from the publisher except in the case of brief quotations embodied in critical articles or reviews.

Legal & Disclaimer

The information contained in this book is not designed to replace or take the place of any form of medicine or professional medical advice. The information in this book has been provided for educational and entertainment purposes only.

The information contained in this book has been compiled from sources deemed reliable, and it is accurate to the best of the Author's knowledge; however, the Author cannot guarantee its accuracy and validity and cannot be held liable for any errors or omissions. Changes are periodically made to this book. You must consult your doctor or get professional medical advice before using any of the suggested remedies, techniques, or information in this book.

Upon using the information contained in this book, you agree to hold harmless the Author from and against any damages, costs, and expenses, including any legal fees potentially resulting from the application of any of the information provided by this guide. This disclaimer applies to any damages or injury caused by the use and application, whether directly or indirectly, of any advice or information presented, whether for breach of contract, tort, negligence, personal injury, criminal intent, or under any other cause of action.

You agree to accept all risks of using the information presented inside this book. You need to consult a professional medical practitioner in order to ensure you are both able and healthy enough to participate in this program.

TABLE OF CONTENTS

INTRODUCTION 1

CHAPTER 1: FUNDAMENTALS OF WOODWORKING 8

CHAPTER 2: PURCHASE YOUR OWN TOOLS 21

CHAPTER 3: GETTING STARTED 39

CHAPTER 4: PLANS FOR WOODWORK 46

CHAPTER 5: EVERYTHING ABOUT CUTTING MORTISE AND TENON JOINTS 53

CHAPTER 6: WOOD WORKED INDOOR FURNISHINGS 62

CHAPTER 7: IN THE WORKSHOP 69

CHAPTER 8: WOOD WORKING 101 76

CHAPTER 9: MAKE TWO CUTS AND MEASURE ONCE. 84

CHAPTER 10: UNDERSTANDING WOOD 91

CHAPTER 11: TOOLKITS TO UTILIZE 103

CHAPTER 12: TOOLS OF THE TRADITIONAL TRADE 124

CHAPTER 13: SELECTING YOUR WOOD 135

CHAPTER 14: BENCHES, CHAIRS, AND STOOLS (INTERMEDIATE PLAN) 146

CHAPTER 15: WOODWORKING PROJECTS 164

CONCLUSION.. 184

Introduction

Hand tools will be the distinction between a standard carcase side as well as an enticing, ready-to-finish side. Flip a dovetail into the London-pattern, which has tails that are too close for any router to access. They transform into a mortise and tenon joint and then into a piston-fit. I'm not saying that you cannot work with wood without any hand tools -- lots of people make

many beautiful items that use electronic equipment only. However, hand tools would be the most useful.

A crucial weapon that liberates your from the limitations on your machine. Perhaps you've felt annoyed by the need to fix the fence of your table saw in small increments? Perhaps, considerably less than 1/16"? Adjusting your inventory according to the proper depth, length and width by handplane allows you to alter your inventory with increments as small to .001".

It could be a child's game to make an instrument, but it's not something you'll need to master for a long time to master. Are you frustrated by the endless amount of evaluation cuts you have to make when putting an mit

Table saw or re saw for an chemical mitre? Do I. It was a source of grieve over the amount of good timber I wasted with these cuts for evaluation.

Knowing how the operation of a backsaw allows users to mark any shape at any angle on nearly any piece of timber, and then cut it the exact dimensions online. This does not mean that you can't.

It is a bit more if it's 90deg or 23.75deg. A handsaw could do

Some convenience. Are you tired of making jigs that are only used once to create some ease?

straight cut, such as cutting off the corners of this foundation of a post-and-frame? A saw and chisel let you earn any size or shape top-quality. Even if each notch may be quite different, you can use your hand to make it.

Tools do not mind. If you can mark it on the timber or cut it in this way. Are you sure to add curves to your project without having to spend time creating many router templates or paying to buy spindle sanders?

A saw, and an appropriate rasp will form any curve you want to imagine in the same way, and you are not limited by the size of the router bit. If you believe in that it is possible to sketch it out and then use a saw, a router could create it. I'm sure that this is all appealing. How else could you possibly have read this book? However, I am sure you are shaky and have fears regarding your job. It's difficult to comprehend. The tools are not available in the United States. The first experiences using hand tools can be difficult. I'm not going say that I am not a good person If you're looking to master the art of sharpening before you can make any progress using planes, chisels or scrapers. If you're able to master this skill (there are many methods to sharpen the instrument, and several of our favorites include in this publication) The benefits will be far more than the time spent learning to create a sharp edge on a piece of steel. As a bonus it will be apparent that learning ways to make chisels sharper can provide you with a wide-ranging view of woodworking that may be a little difficult to grasp by spinning, carving and marquetry. Sharpening your chisel is your entry point to a wider world of woodworking. Once you've started on this path I can assure you that the distinctions between hand tools and power tools will start to blur.

These adjectives"hands" and"energy" might be of less meaning for you when than the phrase they are a change in the word instrument. It is possible to cut Tenons by using the dado stack, and then adjusting to the perfect size using the shoulder plane. You'll be cutting the leg of a cabriole with a smooth band and cut its sinuous curves with the rasp and a document. It is possible to increase the door on the table of your router and align it to the block plane to ensure that it shakes. You can work more efficiently without the need. The efficiency of the work is likely to be a surprise to you. It's not a problem to sand because you'll take less time. It is possible that you want to go back to the shop more than prior to. It doesn't matter if you're conscious of it or not, we are living in a brand new golden age of woodworking that has never been seen before. The cost of machinery is considerably lower when adjusted for inflation as compared to when the time when the Industrial Revolution birthed the business. Any family of any household can afford the Table saw, planer or jointer, which can transform rough lumber into furniture-ready planks. Hand tools have improved in quality than before World War II. For

more than 50 years ago and the best hand instruments were hand-held instruments from the 19th and early 20th centuries.

In order for the old-timers to function, you had to know more about restoration of instruments by removing corrosion, flattening cast iron that is warped, and re-grinding badly damaged chisels. But no longer.

Modern makers such as Veritas, Lie-Nielsen, Clifton, Auriou and Ashley Iles present tools that surpass the capabilities of older tools. They require a few minutes to put in place to use rather than weeks. They're well-constructed using the most modern production methods and steels to compete with other high-end tools in the market. These are, like our equipment, even enjoyable to use. The book that you're holding is the missing link between the hand-hand interaction and machine functionality. The skills and resources listed in this book will be all you require to begin to integrate hand function into machine function.

the tools you can purchase at your local power tool shop. We've carefully selected each chapter to provide this comprehensive guide for how to best switch your woodworking into woodworking. Let's start working.

Chapter 1: Fundamentals Of Woodworking

Woodwork is a broad term and can be quite a complex subject, but here's a straightforward description that enthusiasts are likely to agree with.

Woodworking is an art in which wood is cut and shaped and shaped to make beautiful and useful objects. Woodworking isn't physically demanding and can be done at your own speed. The basics are simple to master, however it's a pastime that's both challenging and new as your skills improve. If you're a lover of solving problems, you'll be a fan of woodworking. I've been doing it for over 40 years and with each new project I design, I have to face new problems. This is an element of my work. It's also a great idea to create amazing things for your home using your hands and your brain. It's generally extremely lonely It is a great hobby when you're a bit more introverted and take on projects from beginning to the end.

Who are the workers? WHO do they represent?

There were two myths about woodworkers.

The shop-teacher who was grumpy and gave youngsters who didn't want be there for a dull lesson, and also the elderly grandfather who sat in his garage for many years to construct birdhouses.

Thankfully this isn't true any more. Woodworking is now more diverse than it ever has before, due to the accessibility of tools and the materials.

In the last 10 years two groups of individuals have made woodworking an enjoyable pastime.

Women first.

First. There wasn't a long time ago that women who worked on wood were uncommon. Women who work with wood are now commonplace. It's impossible to do anything wrong using woodworking.

The second significant demographic growth occurred between 20 and 30. I still encounter people who are employed within areas like the Silicon Valley or have some type of work in the office and are driven to work with their hands.

What is the difference between betting on the "builder" as opposed to "workman? "workman?"

Manufacturer is a fairly new term that was first introduced within the last 10 or so years. It's a general term used to describe those who are interested in working in a variety of fields. We are all makers.

A woodworker is an individual who's main interest is making things from wood and then grinding them. Sometimes, we incorporate other materials, but the main focus remains on wood. It's a cheap, durable material that can be used to easily build.

What is the distinction between woodworking and wildlife?

It's not clear and I like to think of carpenters as building buildings and houses that are built. I can't imagine building houses as a woodworking project made of beams, posts and 2x4s. Woodworking usually refers to the building of furniture and the construction of other items that are moving. However, many people consider woodworkers carpenters, and this isn't a significant distinction.

What is the difference in Cupboard as well as Furniture Making?

There's no real distinction between the two concepts, however cabinetmakers make permanently-installed products like your kitchen cabinets. They mostly work with visible surfaces.

Furniture can be set up wherever the owner would like and other pieces of the piece may, consequently be observed.

The cabinets can use more than the majority of mobilizations of platewood and are supported with screws as well as other mechanical attachments as well as furniture that is made from hardwood and can be assembled with glue and woodwork that is stronger. The manufacturing of furniture may require greater accuracy.

There's plenty of overlap However, there is a lot of overlap. I've made a variety of furniture using screws and furniture, as well as amazing cabinets that rival top-of-the-line furniture.

Woodworking Types

It is possible that you already have an idea of what woodworking is however there are a variety of ways to learn about this skill.

Hand Tool Woodworking

Over the past 20 years, hand tools have experienced an enormous revival. Hand tools are used by woodworkers to create objects with traditional tools and techniques. Scrapers, handsaws and chisels and planes are more suitable to anything that is able to fit into the wall.

Hand tool users are likely to are more connected to the process than other woodworker in the work. It requires patience and an extended learning curve, and you work slower and far less hushed. However, your happiness and satisfaction for you personally can be awe-inspiring.

Power Tool Woodworking

Power tools, such as tables saws and miter saws boxes, and sanders are everywhere and provide an economical way to begin construction projects right away. The cutting of a wooden board on a table does not take piece of the expertise or the precision that a handsaw can bring to.

The most serious drawback of working with power tools is that they could create serious harm. This is not a reason to hinder people from going through the process, however you must be aware of the safety precautions.

Virtual Woodworking

Virtual technologies have been around for some time, but in recent times, they've been priced lower and attracted many more enthusiasts. The most important tool can be described as the CNC machine that makes use of the use of a router to cut precise on wood pieces that are flat. You must sketch out and plan the entire project on a computer. Then, the machine takes care of the rest , and then cuts the pieces. When it's cutting your work, it doesn't need to be at the same location.

Laser cutters or engravers is the second tool that hobbyists use to invest. It allows you to cut more precisely than a CNC, and create gorgeous artwork. The main disadvantages are the cost of digital presses. It is possible to spend a lot of money on them fast. They're not big and you'll likely want table saws as well as other power tools at your shop. Many feel that the digital tools make them feel not feel "connected" with their woodwork, but they prefer to work by hands.

Blended Woodworking

Most people who work in their shop use a mix of hand machines as well as power equipment. For instance, a mixed woodwork technique can make the majority of cuts using the table saw, however an axe can be utilized to make dovetails using hand. Many believe hand tools offer more precision and are able to cut joints that are technical and they enjoy advancing their knowledge in these areas.

Specialty Woodworking

Two kinds of woodwork are made for enthusiasts, typically artists. Scrolling and turning.

Woodturning involves making spindles, cups and other rounded objects using lath. It's similar to carving clay with wooden chisels and the potter's wheel. The only drawback is that lathes can be expensive.

In the typical woodworking shop there are plenty of ways to use both of them, maybe you'll want to create legging tablets or an attractive scrollwork design on a bookcase that looks amazing, however, they're not tools you will frequently use.

Fast Fire-Round Rapid! Are You Safe, Woodworking?

It is probably safer than walking but not as durable as wood. Know how the tools function and how they can be utilized with common knowledge.

Why do you like such amazing works?

Woodworking is a lot of fun and you can build interesting things to decorate your home However, ultimately, it's about finding out our identity and figuring out that life has numerous advantages if we spend the time. Unplug for a few hours each week and turn on the power tools.

Woodworking is depicted in numerous antique Egyptian paintings. A significant amount of Egyptian furniture has been discovered within tombs (such as benches, stools tables, beds, tables and chests). The coffins that were inside the tombs were constructed of wood, too. Woodworking isn't about perfectionism but enjoyment and progress. Woodworking can be a dangerous hobby. Hand tools are typically sharp. If used improperly, they can cause serious injuryor even death.

This kind of project is suited to the school's exhibit extremely well. Students will not just enjoy choosing their mirror or glass inserts and putting it together but also watching how visitors will be impressed by their creations.

When you work in your woodworking workshop Tools aren't the sole risk.

Consider your respiratory system as well. Instruments with the same form and curve's depth can have exactly the same numbers of sweeps as Sheffield regardless of how large or long the shaft is. The more sweeps and the higher the angle of the blade will be.

Jigs are employed to make cuts or holes to improve the precision. They are utilized to coordinate a sequence of cuts that are repeated, so there is no need for regular resets of equipment or pieces of work. Woodworking jigs are helpful in increasing the total duration of an undertaking.

A Review of Wood Working World

Are you ready to begin with a New Hobby? Scrapbooking as well as photography and painting are just some of the many people's interests. However, there's a hobby it was a popular one before the three others. This hobby that has attracted plenty of attention, and is a great option for those who first started it many years back is woodworking.

What else, in addition what is woodwork? Let me first explain the basics of woodcraft in a brief manner. Knowing what tools you have is an essential aspect of wood carving. There's a wide array of tools used in woodwork and they're not only restricted only to the hands. Know your tools and don't underestimate the one's capabilities. Consider that there are there are more than three kinds of wood can be employed to create random wood crafts. As important as looking for woodworking projects, and learning about the techniques involved is knowing what type of wood you're likely to use. If you're just beginning or beginner, it's fine to go with softwood, which means you won't require complex cutting equipment.

In the world of woodworking it is a vast field of possibilities and the best part is that your imagination is working. You are not only able make money but the activity can also be a great way to create a fantastic company.

It requires a amount of imagination and dedication to build a woodworking piece however, it's a lot of fun. Once you've got the whole item in your hand and you'll know that the value of your effort. And the more times you do it the more effective it gets an asset to your efforts.

You can understand how to create things from wood simply by making a decision and starting with it, but if you receive some guidance it will be much easier. A majority of people seek this guidance by visiting the local community college for lessons. Others are more self-sufficient and searching for strategies to improve their career which they can implement at their own speed. A number of these professionally designed plans are online.

Chapter 2: Purchase Your Own Tools

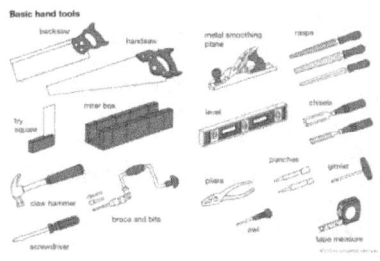

Woodworkers who are just beginning their careers have a lot of mistakes to make when it comes to buying their very first piece of equipment. The first step is to purchase the right equipment.

It is important to decide which tools you'd like to begin with. After that, you'll need to decide on the tools you'll use.

You have a difficult choice. You can buy the most affordable materials from bargain stores and be disappointed with the product later. It is also possible to purchase top quality woodworking materials from specialist shops , which are more expensive. But there's another option that many beginning woodworkers consider: buying hand-tools that are commonly utilized. Garage sales, flea markets or antique club are frequently filled with typical

Hand-crafted equipment that is used for sale at reasonable prices. A four Stanley smoothing plane which retails for $57.50 new in its box can be bought for $15 to $20 in used. Chisels with wooden handles that cost around $10 per new can be purchased for only $5.

There are a few disadvantages when buying used, but. If you're not completely satisfied with the purchase then it's unlikely that you'll be able to obtain an exchange or refund. Some tools are utilized are a requirement

Repair before use. If you follow the suggestions in the following guide, you'll be able to cut down on the amount of time that you spend fixing the old equipment and then immediately put the new ones up to work. Let me start by saying that buying used items isn't an option for everyone. It's unlikely that you're going be able to go to one sale on Saturday morning to complete your store. You'll have to consider. Most people will agree that there's something incredibly appealing when you have a brand-new device. If money is tight and you've some weekends off, it's completely feasible to outfit your store with everything essentials

Imple hand gear, for less than $100.

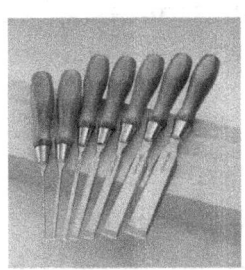

Your Shopping List

Start by determining what you'd like to start with. If you're an instrument enthusiast, you're likely to have to buy around 20 hand tools (till they create an electric scratch and awl). If you intend to perform all your work using hands-on equipment the list below is an excellent place to start and you'll be able to perform a variety of tasks using these tools. The chart below is a great shopping list that includes a few typical flea market bargains we've found across regions like Midwest, South and East. When you begin shopping be sure to bring the list of equipment you require, a high-quality steel ruler that is with inches on it and pen. There are four places to find fantastic used programs auctions and garage sales

There are flea markets and ntique malls. Auctions are great because you might be able to purchase an entire set of equipment to purchase for the price of $20. Because the prices are reasonable it is where most flea market vendors buy tools for selling. Auctions can be lengthy. It is possible to sit for hours waiting for the item you're contemplating to purchase to become for auction. Then you might lose out to a bidder and get a few additional pounds from the pimento

cheese sandwiches that you've eaten. Garage sales are ideal because the person who is who is running them might not be aware of what to charge for the supplies. I've found some great second hand planes at yard sales for only $5. The problem is that you need to travel around town in search of the garage sale, which might or may not have the tools readily available. There are many garage sales that have only a few items for sale.

and a few other tools to choose from. Antique malls on the contrary, are great since there is usually a wide range of options to choose from. But, you must

You will have to cover this convenience. Prices could be higher than those listed here, and there's no opportunity to purchase. I

I'm a fan of flea markets. There are many options to choose from and there's no need to hang for hours, and the prices are lower, particularly when you're willing to bargain.

Chisels

You must have the chisels. From rabbets that pop up to be cut by your router, to the cutting dovetails and paring, they are an absolute necessity. However, used Chisels are hard to locate and are also expensive. The best thing about used chisels is that the majority of them are made of wood handles I'm a huge fan to. The downside of using Chisels is that you're more likely to require milling the cutting edge to fit into an square. I've never seen an old chisel which was not in need of effort. However, don't get too upset about this. A lot of the new chisels you purchase need to be ground again

right out of the box, too. If you're thinking of purchasing a used chisel this is the information you should keep in mind. Begin by stepping the chisel using a ruler made of steel to ensure it's the dimension you'd like to have. Look for chisels that aren't too old-fashioned,

especially specifically on the backside. It's okay to have surface rust but if you find deep pits on the back of the chisel you'll be faced with a lot of maneuvering to do until you are able to get a decent cutting edge. Rust on the front of the chisel is not an issue provided it's not too severe.

The amount of blade remains can be important. As long as the chisel remains one that is a butt one (that is believed to have an

Short blade) short blade), you must have at minimum 3" to short blade), you must have at least 3" to" of blade remaining. If you've had less than that, you may not have any steel that is hardened remaining from the blade and the chisel.

Not able to gain an advantage. Pass. Then take a look the bargain. Do you want to pull the handle away from the socket? If you

could, you're going have to decide whether to fix it or create a new agreement. Follow the same guidelines for mortising chisels. They have been contemplating a sturdier blade without bevels to either. Also, ensure that they are able to endure more punishment such as being hammered with the hammer every day.

A Backsaw, Coping Saw and a Coping

You need a backsaw to cut dovetails and tenons as well as other smaller tasks. Backsaws are called that because they have a rigid backbone, which is clamped onto the back of the blade that makes the blade more rigid through the cutting. Larger backsaws are referred to as Tenon saws. The smaller ones are referred to as dovetail saws. Smaller ones with the round handle are often known as gent's sees. There are many saws, however they typically require a amount of work, such as fixing missing teeth or sharpening. It is best to let a professional do it for you.Dealing saws are very simple instruments that are perfect to cut curves and clea

Nup waste in dovetails. You should ensure that the dovetails you purchase second-hand are completely adjustable. Also you are able to make the blade lock at any angle. Get new blades that contain the same number of teeth at the hardware store for around thirty cents per hour.

Planes

There will be a need for the use of a low-angle block plane to accomplish many things. For instance, if you've glued two pieces of timber , and only one border isn't than the other, the low-angle block plane will be ideal for leveling the joint. There are generally two kinds of block planes that are: the basic old block plane and another is is a low-angle block plane. Block planes are used to hold the blade at 20 degrees one.

The blade on the low-angles is set on 12 different levels. Low-angle planes can reduce the amount of work that a block plane will be to, and work to plan end grain as well as extremely figured woods. Therefore, try purchasing one with a low-angle design if capable of. It is also necessary for this model to have a neck that is flexible. It is the space between the

blade, and the plane's body.

It is also a lot of flexibility as the more open you can make the more tear-out you'll be able to get, especially in the case of guessed woods. To determine if the block plane has an adjustable neck remove the on the front knob of the plane and then try to move the piece of the metal on the side edge of the blade. If the knob moves the neck is adjustable. A different issue is

Block planes from the past are blades are the most common. Begin looking for one that isn't too old and still is still alive. Blades for new block planes are generally 4-1/2" long. If it's smaller

If you're not sure, then you might you'll have If you are, then you might have. Blades that are replacements for certain block planes are difficult to find, especially for those who manufacture oddballs. You are safe use blocks

planes with shorter blades. Examine the plane's underside for flatness. Keep your straightedge -- or border against the edge of the plane, and in some lighter. If you can see important distinctions between the ruler, and only it, you may have to do an entire lot of work to do. The more flat the better.

Another excellent feature of block planes is referred to as"lateral adjustment" This lets you press the blade a little to the left or right side of the rig the right cut. Lateral adjustments aren't exactly identical on every plane, so look for a lever located on the back of the plane, which can move the blade left or right. Smoothing planes are useful for heavier

-duty jelqing. In case you've got a

rough-sawn edge on a plank or plank, a jet plane is able to make it more attractive. It is also possible to make use of it for the final smoothing of rough roug

h-sawn timber. The most well-known planes, specifically the ones built using Stanley h-sawn timber, have the number 4. If you are unable to locate the #4 plane, a #5 might be a good choice as your primary all-purpose plane. Many of the similar principles that block planes are used to probe planes, minus smoothing planes do not have toenails that can be flexed. Instead, they have elastic frogs. The frog's role is to be the part of the

Metal is the art form where the blade remains. Moving the blade forward, you'll be in a position to close the throat. Look for a screw that is frog-like in the back part of your plane. Plans with this screw tend to be a bit flexible, however, it can be an issue to get.

Scrapers

Scrapers are just a small piece of metal with distinctive burrs on them. They function as supercharged sandpaper. They can make tabletops more flat and reduce the squeeze-out of glue. I've yet to see an old model available. Buy a new model. It is also necessary to buy mill bastard files and a burnisher in order to kickstart your scraper. Mill bastard files are likely to be identified as the same. Burnishers look like a magic metallic wand that has wooden grip.

Blend

Mix squares are the constant friend of this woodworker. It is able to lay joints out along the plank's edge and draw 45-degree mit

Make sure you have res on all your devices. Make sure you are cautious once you buy one. I typically start looking for a Starrett brand square foot. They are more expensive ($25 used, $57 new) however, they're worth every penny. Other sections can be serviced when money is scarce.

. Here's what you need to look for.

The first step is to ensure that the square remains square. The square should be placed from an edge small piece of wood, and mark an outline.

Turn the square over and draw another line that is close to the first. If the lines are in identical then the lines are parallel.

When your square is square. Otherwise, move. Be sure to

The blade can be secured securely. If you come across one that is able to pass these tests but fails to pass these tests, don't consider buying it. Instead, buy it.

Perfect squares can be difficult to come across.

Marking Gauge

The judge who signals lays out mortises, screws, and other such things. A pin at the ends of this judge marks the timber, while the mind determines where the mark is made. Find the marking gauge by with a snare, which is not ground out of the ground. S

Ome indicators have two hooks. They're perfect for setting out mortises and Tenons. If you can find one, it is a good idea.

If you can, think of it a benefit. Also, ensure that you have the ability to keep the weapon in place around the beam.

Sliding Bevel Gauge

These helpful devices allow you to shift angles from one place to another. For instance, suppose you want to align the table saw at an exact angle that matches the work. Attach the bevel gauge to the angle that is appropriate to your project and secure the blade. The gauge should be set from onto the saw's blade, and then tilt it until it's in the same direction.

completely against the judge of the right. There are two elements to look for. First, make sure the blade isn't congested or bent. You want it to be as perfect as possible. Second, you must be honest.

It is a given that you are able to lock the blade in a secure way so that it doesn't transfer when you knock it a bit.

Bargaining

People like to haggle, while others would not even consider it when buying automobiles. I'm not interested, but I'll always find the best price from two methods -- and not even be rude. First, suppose they'll pay 15 to 20% for various things, and then give the same amount. If a plane costs 25 dollars, provide them with $20. They'll always take the amount. Second, buy some things from the same retailer.

Usually, the cost becomes more adaptable. I

The plane cost $25 and a 25 mix square and the estimate of $8% for around 40 to 31 percent away. Another point: sales at flea markets typically increase as they get closer to the time of stopping. The chances are not as wide, however should you be well-funded and a trader isn't required to carry the items to start his next batch. There is a chance that you will be lucky.

Chapter 3: Getting Started

If you've never dealt with wood before, you could find the thought of working with wood quite intimidating. You'll not only need to cover all the wood and tools that you require and you'll need to learn new skills as well. The good thing is that once you master basic skills, you'll discover that the rest of the abilities will be mastered easily. When you begin working on wood, be aware that that you'll be able to master all the aspects of woodworking. There are a variety of skills available, and various woods must be used in various ways. It's likely that you'll never be done learning, and that's been considered a good choice as it will doubt keep you entertained. Woodworking can be an extremely engaging hobby with the potential of leading to the profession of your choice in the future, if that's your goal. If you're careful and do what you're told to do and don't take any unnecessary risks, you'll be able to have a great time woodworking for years to be.

Being Secure

No matter if you've been working with wood for all of your life or are looking to take woodworking up as a passion It is essential to ensure that you are safe. That means you must take into account the possibility of dangers when doing work that involves woodwork, and you'll have to be patient with the work you're doing. Many accidents have happened due to individuals who hurry their work or believing that accidents will never happen to them. Every day, accidents happen all over the world If you're not cautious you might be at the center of one. Take precautions, make every effort to stay clear of accidents, and your woodworking experience can be much more enjoyable. Here are some tips that can help you be safe now and later when you are able to fine-tune your abilities:

Use the appropriate equipment

Most crucial ways to protect yourself is to use the correct safety gear. It is recommended that you don't take out a woodworking tool without wearing at the very least the minimum safety equipment. It is recommended to consider purchasing and making use of:

Latex gloves are particularly useful in the case of applying finishing

Protection for your ears - when making use of routers, planers and other tools that are loud

Safety glasses are required to be worn all the time

Of course, there's plenty of safety equipment to choose from but the 3 above items are the minimum you must have and use when appropriate.

The correct attire

Each time you step the foot into your workplace it is important to wear the appropriate attire.

Beware of wearing loose fitting clothing because they could catch on cutter heads or blades.

Do not wear necklace chains, bracelets as well as any jewelry that hangs because they could also get stuck in equipment

Wear comfortable clothes throughout the day However, wearing clothing that can also protect your body from the wood chips which could cut through light fabric.

Do not drink and work

Alcohol consumption prior to or during the time you work is extremely risky. It may be tempting to sip a little alcohol on the weekend as working, but believe me when I say that it can harm your judgment. If you're not drinking it is also important to be sure to avoid using drugs as well, as they may affect your judgment. If your judgment and concentration are impaired and you're less likely to get injured in an accident. You should wait until you've finished your work for the day prior to deciding whether or not you want to off a glass of delicious stuff.

Switching off the power

If you begin working using tools, you might often find one with some sort of blade or bit that requires replacement. If this happens, ensure that you switch off the power prior to doing anything else. Switch off the power on the wall so that there's no way for electricity to enter even if happen to knock the switch. By taking a few extra precautions to ensure your safety could mean that you'll be able to protect your toes, fingers.

Make use of only one extension cord

I've learned from personal experiences that it's very easy to trust an array of extension cords. The problem with this is that you're likely to forget that your equipment is hooked up. The reason for using only one cord is that you'll need to shut off the device that you're not currently making use of.

Beware of blunt cutting tools

You might be wondering why I've asked to take this step and I'm sure you'll be shocked by how many people make use of blunt tools. If you're using the wrong instrument that's less sharp than it should be, you'll need work harder to finish the task.

If you're forced to put in more effort than you really need to is likely that the equipment you're using could create a kick-back or bind which can be risky. Make sure that your blades are clean, and you'll take less time while delivering better results.

Keep an eye out for anything made of metal.

When you're cutting wood, please be aware of metal because it might get stuck within the wood and that's what could create a serious problem. Make sure you take a close inspection of the wood you're planning to cut, so that you are able to see all metal (Such as nails, stapes and screws) and take them out before they cause issues.

Do not get distracted.

It's not easy to stay clear of distractions in any area of your life and this is especially the case when working on wood. If you need to take a break from what you're doing, be sure to turn off any equipment you're using. If you must complete a cut, complete it before doing anything else because rushing or having to return to the cut could lead to problems.

Chapter 4: Plans for Woodwork

If you're truly attracted to woodworking and would like to be successful in it then you need to be able to follow plans in all instances. It is impossible to create anything if you don't have a plan. You're likely to fail in even the simplest task, which is wasted time and money. Professional woodworkers and skilled craftsmen must follow a specific plan always, since they are aware that the process will go much more smoothly and more smooth and they are likely to avoid mistakes when following a particular strategy.

Every plan should state what type of project you're planning to tackle, whether it's challenging, easy or moderate. It should also outline the tools you'll require to complete the project, and the supplies. Then , it will guide you in how to complete the job done.

Here's a sample plan that can provide you with an idea of what that you need to think about when planning your next woodwork project

A portable Shop Table

Difficulty Level

Woodworking is easy

Ending

Staining or paint is optional

Time to Finish

3-4 hours

Tools Essential

Power Drill

Circular Saw

Layout Square

Materials Required

Ten (10) 2x4 8 feet long

Four (4) 1x6 8-feet long

A single (1) sheet of 4x8 of 1/2-inch CDX Plywood

A single (1) 4-x8 sheet 1/4-inch of Masonite

Four (4) 3-inch Spring Door Hinges

Four (4) 3-inch Door Hinges

Four (4) Three-inch Casters

Four (4) 1 inch closed eye Hooks (screw-type)

(2) 6-foot lengths of small nylon rope. (2) 6' lengths nylon rope of small size

2-1/2 inches and 1-1/2 inches Deck Screws

Glue

Method

The table's base:

A simple butt-joint design. It should be 96 by 44 inches in dimensions.

Cut the two longer sides of base-2x4's up to 89-inches long.

Make one 2x4 cut in two (2) pieces of 44 inches for the two sides of the table's base.

Create Three (3) 41 inches pieces of two additional 2x4's. These are the three stringers providing strength to the table.

Make the table top and make sure that you have at least 2-1/2 inch screws on each joint to ensure that it's solid. Be sure the table's surface is rectangular.

Add legs to the base

Cut the 4 1x6's into eight pieces. Each one should be 35-1/4 inches in length.

- With the base laid down on its side, secure two pieces of 1x6 on each side. Utilizing a square, make sure that they are fixed in a 90-degree angle. The first leg should be in a straight line with the corner, and the other one is in a position to overlap the first.

Stringers that are attached

Stringers attached to tables' legs ensure stability and strength.

2. Cut two 2x4's into the length of 92 inches

Cut one 2x4 in two parts, with each measuring measuring 44 inches long

Note where the stringers will be set on the table's legs using your pencil

Attach them by putting one-quarter screws and into the stringer.

The table should be turned to feel its power.

Attaching the caster board to the table

This is accomplished by putting the table on its feet

- Make the stock to support the casters. Cut the 2x4 into two lengths of 43-1/2 inches.

Attach two hinges to the edges of the caster board. After they're done the caster board will be able to move freely in a 90-

degree arc and remain straight as the table gets set down.

Connecting the base braces of the caster to the stringers

The braces should be able to secure the caster's base in its down position. They must be secured using spring hinges. It is possible to use cut offs by cutting stringers or you can cut a new 2x4 to fix them.

Attach the tables with casters using the table turned upside down.

Attach a caster at either end of the using 1 1/2 inch screws. After you've finished you can test whether the table is able to roll effortlessly when in the correct place.

Connect an extension rope to the braces of the caster. It will lift the braces of your caster up to allow the table to sit on its legs while you work on it.

Connect the top of table

- Put the plywood of 1/2 inch on the base of the table, keeping the table in the correct place. Be sure to place it in the correct the correct position.

Attach the top to the base using 1 1/2 inch screws. Don't use glue at this time.

Then, place the Masonite top on the plywood. It is a re-usable item when it wears out. It is recommended that the Masonite should be level against the plywood along all four sides.

Attach the one-inch screws plywood's base as well as to the table's base, so you don't have screw ganging at the base of the table.

It is set and you can paint it or stain it, excluding the Masonite to give the table a more attractive appearance and also to shield it from grime, dirt and water.

When you go through every stage of the process It is easier to monitor the progress made and make sure that everything you require to start are accessible.

Chapter 5: Everything About Cutting Mortise and Tenon Joints

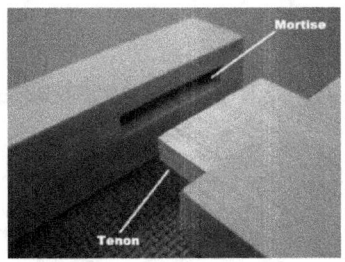

Once you have an understanding of the basics the process of milling the board and are able to mill a board, we will explore ways to improve this fundamental method. This chapter will concentrate on what exactly mortise and Tenon joints are and how to make these joints. Let's get started.

What is Mortise? What is the Tenon?

If you're conscious of it or whether you are, mortise and tenon joints are the most commonly used technique for cabinetry and furniture work in the present. As opposed to trying to clarify the fundamental construction of these two types of cuts that are unique you should first to provide an image, which can be found below.

It is evident in the image above The mortise cut is the "female" portion of the cut. Likewise, the tenon could be described as being the "male" part that is cut. The main reason the mortise cuts are so well-liked by cabinet and furniture makers is the expansion and contraction of wood as time passes. Did you realize that the structure of wood changes in time without any intervention? This is one of the main reasons why designs for pocket jigs are generally viewed as flawed due to the fact that the design of a pocket jig usually does not adequately take into account the expansion and contraction of the wood that it will be experiencing. However, this is not the case with mortise and tenon joints. If the image above seems at present a bit daunting don't allow it to be. The cuts of this kind are quite simple to make.

Step 1: Cut Your Mortise Joint First

If you're considering cutting both the mortise and Tenon joint, the best tip is cutting the mortise first as it will be simpler to alter the tenon joint so that it fits inside the mortise joint instead of attempting to fit the mortise joint to the tenon joint after you've constructed the tenon. In addition, the standard principle of the tenon joints is it is approximately about four-five times as thick as the tenon while the actual tenon should be half what the width of your board. It is quite easy to determine, and can be observed in the image above.

When cutting your mortise, then you're likely to require the router table was discussed in the prior chapter. You'll need to set up this table with a certain type of bit. And this kind of bit is referred to as an up-spiral bit. An illustration showing an up-spiral bit can be found below.

It is evident in the image above the tool seems to be round and flat all at once. The roundness of the tool permits it to cut the wood, and the edge that is flat provides the flatness you see in the image of the mortise that was cut.

Step 2: Move Towards Cutting Your Tenon Joint

Similar to what we used to do with the mortise joints and the mortise joint, we'll also turn to the router table in order we can cut Tenons in the same way like mortise joints. To make this type of cut the tool you'll need is the slot-cutting tool. The slot-cutting bits is shown in pictorial format below.

It is evident in the photo as you can see from the image, the slot-cutting knife is going to pierce the wood piece and allow it to have that space to breathe. It will also enhance the mortise cut you've probably already made. It's obvious that the table used for routers is designed possible for these cuts to be very simple to create, provided you are able to take measurements and ensure that the work you're doing is executed in a precise method. Mortise and Tenon joints are generally thought of as being one of the oldest methods of making furniture in the woodworking industry This is the reason it's crucial to learn how to cut these pieces when you are aware that making furniture is something you'll be interested in.

The Three Basic Types of Joints: Mortise and Tenon

Once you have an understanding of what mortise tenon joints are , and how to go about making them using the router table we're going to take a look at three of the most common kinds of mortise and joints you can make. These types of joint include the stopped/blind through and the an angled mortise & tenon joint. Let's look at each of these.

The Tenon Joint and the Stopped/Blind Mortise

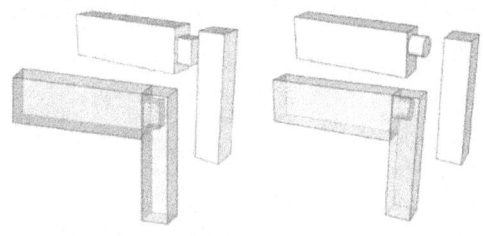

The mortise that is stopped or blind and the tenon joint is the kind of joint - mortise and Tenon that we observed in the first image in this chapter. This joint received its name because of its tenon appears to be "blind" when it has been snugly fitted into its companion mortise. The image below illustrates the concept a little more clear.

In the image above, you'll notice in the above image the tenon has been hidden from the view of the public. It is also important to remember that the tenon doesn't need to be square. It can instead be circular, as the image illustrates. If you continue to pursue the woodworking hobby it is likely that you will be able to begin making circular tenon joints however, the design of circular tenon joints is out of the topic of this article for right now.

The through Mortise and Tenon Joint

The picture above shows the through mortise and Tenon joint is named because this kind of joint passes through the furniture piece that is being discussed. In the image above the mortise is a part of the leg of the table and the tenon most likely a an element of the frame supporting the other parts of the table together.

It is the Angled Mortise and Tenon Joint

The final kind of mortise and joint we'll be looking to take a look is the angled mortise joint. If you've ever sat outside on a scorching summer day in an Adirondack chair and you're aware of the angle mortise as well as the tenon joint, whether you are aware of the difference or not. A picture of an angled mortise as well as the tenon joint is shown below.

The angled mortise and Tenon joint is more sophisticated over the previous two kinds of mortise and tenon joints we have discussed in this chapter. However, once you've been able to build a successful kind of joint, you are able to proceed to build other kinds of joints in the way you'd like. We hope that this chapter given you the impression that you're competent in designing a specific kind of joint for your needs. As you'll see when you grasp the fundamentals and the process, everything else is a matter of the form of a fairly straightforward step-by-step method.

Chapter 6: Wood Worked Indoor Furnishings

Good furniture can be difficult to locate. It is also possible that the price likely isn't the best. However, if you are unable to find the perfect furniture in the stores, you can create something even more unique by creating these yourself. In this section, we will show you some of the most beautiful furniture made of wood that you can find.

Kitchen Table

To build an individual kitchen table you should begin by building the base. Or more precisely the part which will be used as the table. It is necessary to have three 2x4's for this job. Set the 2 x 4's in a row, side-by-side before drilling holes through the exterior of one of the boards towards the interior of the board next to it. These holes are known as "pocket holes" and serve to connect the two wood pieces. That's exactly what we'll accomplish here.

The next step of the project will be to use wood screws and place them into the pockets for fastening the two x 4's. Then run a jointer across the wood until they are as smooth and flawless you're unable to tell that they were initially three separate sections of timber.

After the table is put in place, it is time to build the table's legs. Get another piece of 2x4 wood and cut legs that approximately 2 feet in length and about 4 inches wide. When these dimensions are created from the wood, they can be set over your table. pockets can be created by drilling holes through the table's top legs as well as the table for screwing into the right place.

In the same way similar to the way you did it before you drill into the outside edge of the of the table leg, and then up into the table, before inserting woodworking screws to securely attach tables to legs.

Take a saw blade and cut each notch around 1/4 inch. Then repeat the process on the cross-beam using the cross-beam as a bridge to join both assemblies. Take an electric drill. go through the cross beam, and then into each leg. You can here as well, put in wood screws to anchor the legs.

After the legs have been attached and the legs are in place, sandpaper is rubbed across the table to make sure that any uneven edges are smoothed. In the end, you can apply wood varnish in order to create a table that is bit more appealing visually. That's it to it. Your kitchen table is now complete.

The Living Room Coffee Table

Every home should have the coffee table in the living room. It's where we host guests, it's where we place our drinks after a long day at work. It's also the central piece for our most private moments of rest. Therefore, it's important to be able to have a piece of furniture that will enhance the various activities. This woodworking project will accomplish exactly this.

To build this table, all you need is a 3-by-4-foot piece of plywood that serves as the base for your table. Then, take 2 x 4s and cut them to lengths that are sufficient to completely cover the plywood but short enough not to leave any visible overhang.

Once you've made the boards use a power drill and drill holes in the ends of the boards approximately half an inch away off the surface. Then, grab some wood screws and attach the boards to the plywood using the freshly made holes.

Once you've done this, make sure you take a 2 x 4 and cut it into four equally cut pieces. These will form the legs of your coffee table. Turn the table's upside down and place each leg on corner of table. Drill diagonal holes through each leg, passing through the leg and table.

Lastly, join the legs using wood screws, and your table is completed. Now you can sand your table, and then apply the varnish to the table as much that you feel is needed. Once you've completed all this the furniture is set to use.

Rustic Table Lamp

Everyone could benefit from a table lamp that is well-lit. What night , while you read your favourite book is incomplete without it? The latest novel and the dependable lamp bulb are a perfect match. There are numerous other applications for this ubiquitous but highly useful piece of furniture.

So, without further delay this is how to rock your table lamp to impress! All you require to create your lamp is a simple 1 2 x 2 board. Make the 1 x 2 and make use of an electric saw split the board into 2 equal parts. Then, use one of the pieces for the base. Take another piece, and set it on the other end of the base. drill two diagonal holes into the corner, running through the outer part of one piece and inside the other.

These are pockets, through which you can connect the boards. Inside these holes, fix the base with two screws for woodworking. Then, you will need to cut a 3 inch hole through the middle of the upright part on the bottom. This is the place to place the bulb. Simply run your extension cord through the outlet to connect the light bulb, and your authentic tale lamp is now ready!

Chapter 7: In The Workshop

In the previous chapters, we dealt with a number of crucial aspects of woodwork. Now you have the tools you'll need along with your wood and idea for your woodworking project. Where do you go to complete everything? Yes, in the workshop.

Consider all the places you believe would be ideal for your workshop An outbuilding is an option better that an attic and a basement. The attic is not an ideal location for carrying the materials and artwork to and from the stairs. However the basement is likely to be damp and dark. It also makes the noise more alarming to those living in the home.

If you do not have a location that you can set up your workshop outside of your home Try to locate a spot that is well-lit (both for the sake of your eyes as well as your work). Also, the area must be dry, otherwise your tools will get rusty and the work will be damaged. Finally, a location where the temperature can be maintained (of course, nobody would ever want to work in harsh environments).

The door of your workshop must be secured by a lock it, in order to protect young children from being injured, to stop your work from getting destroyed while you're out of the building or making your work and also to stop the use of your tools to serve domestic needs.

It is also important to have something on when you're working: overalls and an apron for work (made out of strong cloth, such as ticking or denim) with pockets in it and when you've got long days of dirty work ahead of you, switching your clothing to the latest clothes you've got around could be a good idea. They are more comfortable than the general attire when it is warm.

You could also engage an architect or carpenter to design your shop for you or do it yourself. When you are done the first item you'll need is a work bench.

A workbench may be easy to build, yet it can be extremely beneficial over the long haul. To build your first workbench, you can follow these steps to construct it yourself , or hire someone else to build it for you (it's really your decision).

First, you'll need an drill, screw bit set along with a saw, and a carpenter's square so that all cuts aren't distorted or bent. In addition you will also require things to transport materials to and from the place you're creating your work bench.

You'll need 2x4s to frame the frame as well as 4x4s on the legs. Get the strongest wood you can (at minimum 3/4" is suggested). Buy 3 inches (7.6 centimeters) wood screws. These are what will join the frame and the top. For the frame, construct an oval out of 2x4s. This will serve as your countertop. To ensure strength, place an L-bracket at every corner. If it's still an square, you might need to install and strengthen your reinforcement with 2x4's. The quantity of materials and their size will depend on the size of your table and workspace However, you could opt to build the countertop approximately 36 inches (91.4 cm) from the surface. It is also possible to attach it to the wall.

To build your legs, you can make them using 4x4s or 2x4s in case you are not making use of them for heavy duty reasons. Next, put down sheets of plywood over the square. This is your countertop. Attach them to the square with screws. Connect the legs to your square, and also to the wall, if you wish. It is suggested to use L brackets to ensure the legs don't wobble.

If you'd prefer to use an additional shelf beneath the countertop for 18 inches (45.7 cm) above the floor. If the workbench is intended for use in heavy duty It is suggested to place two 2x4 laterally or width way (or both) underneath your countertop at least every 18 inches to provide support. A tip is to always drill your holes in order to ensure that the wood doesn't split.

Following the workbench is the bench-vise. It's basically an additional pair of hands to aid you in your work. If you are a beginner's bench-vise you can follow these steps to build it yourself or hire someone else to build it for you (again it's your choice)

You'll need materials: wooden board metal brackets, screws wood glue, four small vices made of metal.

Start by making jaws (some bench vises are made out of cast iron , and are easily bolted to the top of a work bench to offer the features you require). Cut a 24 inch long 2-by-4 into four equal pieces . two pieces will be placed horizontally, while the rest lay horizontally perpendicular with the horizontal pieces. The pieces are glued together using wood glue in two L-shaped shapes. Once you've joined the pieces of wood then use the metal brackets to help strengthen and support the wooden pieces (the brackets should be able to fit in the L-shape, and create jaws made of wood that are more solid).

Once you've got your jaws made of wood for your bench vise it's now simple to complete the project with the clamp vises made of metal. Secure each of the boards that are horizontal in place using two clamp vises. Now you can move the jaws of the adjustable wooden to any position you want by moving them. Make sure, once you are in the right place, you make sure to tighten the vises made of metal.

Also, you must have something in the front of the bench-top that you can press on your work for planning and so on. Also known as the bench-stop. The simplest method is to make use of two screws (screwed into the hole so that they project around a quarter inch and is adjustable as required). Also, there is the wooden stop, which comes with the advantage of not causing scratches on the surface of wood. Other people may also use a tiny piece of wood with a V-shaped slit at the other end (to keep boards in place or to hold joists to plan).

A few old-fashioned bench-stops are comprised of a piece made of wood that is about one or two inches in size that is fixed very securely to at the base of the bench. It can slide up and down using a propeller from the mallet or the hammer.

You may also opt to have a different bench that to utilize when painting and varnish (a finishing bench).

Chapter 8: Wood Working 101

Woodworking is an enjoyable hobby. Additionally, it's an actual skill. You can apply it to make money or begin your own company.

The advantages of Woodworking

Here are just a few of the benefits of starting woodworking:

It will help you save money.

A piece of furniture could cost you the equivalent of a leg and an arm. If you're looking to cut costs It's a good idea to create the furniture you want. Woodworking can save you between $50 and $300 per piece. In reality, the majority of the plans for woodworking that are included in this book are priced lower than 50 dollars.

It provides you with a powerful feeling of fulfillment.

Making your own woodworking projects is a huge accomplishment. It will give you satisfaction. It also gives you bragging rights as you can inform your friends "I created that".

It's a wonderful way to pass the time.

If you are looking for a rewarding hobby you can do woodworking as an idea to consider. It's actually quite enjoyable and relaxing. Therefore, instead of sitting in front of the TV and wasting time, why not be productive like creating your own study table or stool.

You can master the latest ability.

Woodworking is an art which can be used to create a successful company or begin your career in the field of furniture. It's similar to learning a new language, or learning how make food or baking.

It can improve your overall health.

Research has proven that woodworking can have positive health benefits. It boosts your mental function since you have to apply reasoning when designing and implementing woodworking plans. It also aids in preventing depression since it creates a the feeling of accomplishment.

Woodworking can also increase your muscle tone , and helps improve your overall bone health. It improves joint flexibility and increases your balance. It also assists in controlling your weight and boosts the cardiovascular system. It can help lower blood pressure, and is an effective stress-management tool.

Woodworking can also be a good exercise. It will help you burn off calories. Strengthen your muscles and increase your metabolism.

It is a viable way to earn money.

When you have improved your skills in woodworking as you progress, you could begin making money selling wood work. This is a fantastic source of income, and you could earn lots of money through this.

What is the best way to choose the right Woodworking Project

There are many things to take into consideration when deciding on the best woodworking project. These include:

Budget

What is the amount you are willing to invest in an undertaking in woodworking? If you're on a strict budget, you might want to create rustic stools and decorations at first. These projects can be cheaper to finish since you'll make use of scrap materials.

Time

For the majority of newbies, woodworking is just an activity to do. It is therefore crucial to know the amount of time you can spend on your project. If you're building something that's simple like a floating shelf , or an wine rack, you'll only require between one and three hours. However, if you're making something more complex, like a bed, or a desk, you'll require at least a day to finish the task.

Skill Level

Also, you should consider your ability level when selecting the appropriate project. It is best to choose simple woodworking projects like the wine holder, stool as well as a basic study table.

The need

Naturally, you need to figure out what type of woodworking task you require. Do you need a brand new chair or bed?

Tips for Measuring

Woodworking is quite like life. The best way to learn is through experiences. However, the most effective measurement advice you'll ever hear is "measure twice and cut twice".

Here are some useful measurement tips can be used:

Select the tape measure that is right for you.

There are many varieties of tape measure, like surveyors tape measure, pocket tape measures measuring specialist tape, keyring tape measure and Auto lock tape measures and numerous others. If you're working with wood it is recommended to make use of a tape measure that includes feet and inch marks. Be sure that the marks are simple to understand. Be sure to eliminate any extra markings that might create confusion.

Then, you can burn an inch.

The majority of tape measures have the ends of the tapestress riveted, typically in the range of an inch or less. To get an precise measurement, it is recommended to melt one inch. That means you'll need begin measuring at the 1 inch mark.

Don't bend the measuring tape.

If you're measuring a corner make sure you don't bend it because this can result in an incorrect measurement. You should take separate measurements of the vertical and horizontal line.

Follow the steps.

For the beginner, it's best to follow the plan for woodworking completely. In time you'll be able modify the plans a to modify it to your liking.

Make use of a marker or pencil.

It is important to have a marker or pencil. It will be simpler cutting wood pieces with greater precision. Utilize a ruler to make sure your line is straight.

Also, make sure you invest in high-quality measuring tools since in woodworking, measurement is the most important thing.

Choosing Your Workspace

Garages can be used or basement to create a work space. However, if you wish to make your passion into a business then you could create a workspace in the backyard of your home. Your work space must be secure and must be enclosed so that you do not be disruptive to your family and your friends by making a lot of sound.

Woodworking can be exciting and fun and also a lot of fun. What's the chance? Perhaps, your skills in woodworking could be the key to getting to a new career and into the business world.

Chapter 9: Make Two Cuts and Measure Once.

Many woodworkers give little consideration to the majority of the tools they have at their disposal, as they are too busy selecting the best tools, such as chisels, scrapers special jigs hands planes and tools tools for woodworking, as well as all kinds of tools to make their work easier and with greater precision. What they're not focusing on is measuring and marking instruments.

Look over what you've got in the way of measuring and marking instruments. Most of the typical issues in woodworking stem from the use of four-sided figure frames and joints, casework, or joint that are not properly fitted and so on. and can be traced back to marking and measuring mistakes. The perpetrator usually is an issue of using an incorrect marking and measuring instrument to accomplish the task. Tape measures were not used to make the extremely precise measurements that lots of woodworking projects require.

When it comes to woodworking jobs the first thing you need must do is measure the linear measurement and marking it. Incorrect calculations as small as the 100th percentile marking and measuring in complicated joinery or small pieces of solid wood are likely tolater show up as gaps in joints or uneven parts, or any other undesirable outcomes.

The degree to which you have the capability to interpret a measurement an accurate marking on the piece wood, it is the result of taking measurements from point 1 to point 2. A tape measuring device in order to make an exact measurement is often a challenge because measuring tapes aren't intended to be laid flat. A precise and easy to understand measuring and marking instrument is essential for any woodworking task.

Regulations and Tape Measures

Since even the most efficient measuring instruments aren't expensive and many woodworkers can afford various tape measures and rules that meet various needs. It is, however, recommended to use the same measuring instrument or rule throughout the project to ensure that there's any difference between one device and the other. Purchase both tape measures and rules that have standard and metric graduations- but be sure to not confuse one with the other after you've started to identify a piece of work. It is possible to measure a single piece of wood accurately and then use it as a model to design the other pieces in the event that more than one of the same dimensions is needed. This will save you time in the measurement and marking process.

1. Tape measure- retractable steel tapes that range between 6 and 16 feet (2 to 5m) in length, are typically separated along both sides. The lock button can stop

the immediately retracting of the tape. Some tapes come with an LCD screen with liquid crystals that tell you the distance at which the tape was actually removed from the case. an integrated memory stores the measurement when you pull back the tape. Self-adhesive steel tapes can be found without cases that can be affixed to the top edge of your workbench.

2. Fourfold rule- The Carpenter's rule that folds, made of boxwood, with capes at the end and brass hinges remains popular among traditional artists. Many folding rules are 3 feet (1m) long and completely extended. Since wood is fairly dense, you must put a rule of wood on an edge in order to accurately transfer measurements onto the work. Rules made of plastic can be, in certain instances, constructed using diagonal edges to avoid this issue.

3. Straightedge-- every workshop should have at least one strong metal straightedge. It should be between 1ft 8in

and 6-in in length. A straight edge that is diagonal is ideal for precise cuts with the marking knife, as well as for testing whether a planed surface is totally flat. Certain straightedges can be engraved using standard metrics or graduations.

T-Bevels and Squares

Squares are employed to ensure that the things are in a perfect position relative to one another. In a woodshop, such things might include an tenon shoulder edge of the board or the jointer fence. However, a square is an abstract concept. If you look at it carefully enough there is nothing that truly square. Certain things seem to be larger than other things. There are three types of squares used when working with wood.

1. Try squares are among the most commonly used squares for furniture makers. They are made up of blades of brass or steel (typically between 6 and 12 inches long) embedded in a more robust

wood or metal stock. If the stock is wood, it has to be covered with metal in order to ensure that it is durable and precise. The reliability of the try squares may differ significantly, even between those manufactured by the same manufacturer.

2. Engineer's squares are similar in design to the test squares, but they are constructed entirely from steel. Blade lengths start at around 2 inches. The squares that are designed for engineers are more reliable than try squares, possibly since engineers are a much more demanding group than woodworkers. Engineer's squares may be used in conjunction with try squares.

3. Framing squares-they were designed for the construction of houses. They come with two big blades that form an ideal angle. The first blade measures 2in wide by 24in long, the one that is 1 1/2 inches by 18in in length. Framing squares can't be counted as accurate engineers' squares or even try using squares.

Marking Tools

1. Pencils-Each retailer requires pencils to draw your designs on and mark wood in order to keep track of joints and what part is joined where.

2. Knives are essential in a woodshop to perform tasks like cutting cardboard templates or marking shoulders of tenons. You can pick from a range of knives. Box cutters and pocket knives, as well as utility knives that retract their blade are all helpful at a woodworking shop.

3. Awls-These are pointed, pointy instruments that serve a variety of uses. They differ in their sharpness as well as their shaft's thickness. A fine-pointed awl is ideal to draw lines and mark joints. A broad-pointed, thick-shanked awl can be ideal for making small pilot holes into wood prior to drilling. The dimple it creates when tapping with a mallet makes the precise starting place for the drill part.

Chapter 10: Understanding Wood

Wood is the primary component in woodworking. It is essential to are aware of the appropriate kind of wood for your work. This chapter will go over everything there is to know about the wood used in woodworking.

Wood Structure Types

Wood is a must for woodworking. Even though the majority of hobbyists begin using plywood, it's crucial to be aware of hardwoods if you plan to go to work with fine wood. It is crucial to note that all hardwoods contain vessels used for creating sap. But, the size and location of these vessels may impact the porosity of wood. This article will talk about the different types of structural hardwood.

Ring Porous

This kind of structure has the largest pores found in beginning of the wood, and the smaller pores more dispersed towards the center and the center. This kind of timber is referred to "open-grained" wood. Since it has pores that are larger in the earlywood, but smaller pores in the latewood, there is an uneven distribution of stain into the wood. Specific species that have this kind of wood structure are oak and Ash.

Semi-ring porous

Also known as semi-diffuse porous this kind of wood structure has big pores within the earlywood , and small ones within the laterwood. It is not characterized by the distinct zone found in ring-porous woods. The species that exhibit this kind of wood structure are cottonwood, black walnut, and butternut.

Diffuse Porous

The pores are evenly distributed throughout the wood's early as well as the latewood. There is no difference. The pores are smaller and because the distribution is uniform the absorption of stain is also equal. This kind design of structure for wood is known as closed-grain wood. The most common examples of porous diffuse woods are maple, cherry, and yellow poplar.

Non-porous

Non-porous woods don't have vessels, but water is carried in the living tree known as tracheid cells. This is why wood with this design appears slimmer. Examples of non-porous timbers include various varieties that are pines.

How do you determine the quality of Wood

There are various kinds of woods that you could begin woodworking with. If you're just beginning and are looking for the best kind of wood could be a challenge. This article will provide information on what you should look for in a lumber selection to use for woodworking.

Find out if there are any Defects

When selecting woods it is essential to check if they are defective. The cause of the defect is the imperfections in the log and the excessive presence of it may impact your woodworking project. The imperfections are caused by bugs, fungus, or sometimes lightning strike. While this doesn't mean you have to try to avoid wood that has defects however, you must at the very least begin working with high-quality wood so that you do not encounter a lot of issues while beginning in woodworking.

Find out if the Wood has a Bow

A bow is the curve of your wood as you put it in the vertical point. One bow is fine, however if the wood is adorned with many bows, it is best to stay clear of it.

Watch for Twists

In addition to looking for bows, it's crucial to check for twists. A twist is regarded as an indication of warping the wood. This is the time when wood gets twisted and makes it difficult to work with.

Look For Cupping

Cupping is a form of warping that occurs when the wood is curved through the length of wood. It typically occurs in stock with one inch thickness. It is possible to reduce the amount of cupping making use of a planer for the surface, however in cases where the amount of cupping is significant then a planer is not the solution.

Beware of Wood with Crooks

Crooks are a natural phenomenon caused by the development of the tree. Crooks can only be found only on just one edge of the tree and when they do be on the edges of the stock it is easy to take it away.

Examine for cracks

Small cracks are not a problem. But, it is usually a sign of the presence of stress in the wood fibers as a result of drying. Avoid purchasing stocks with small cracks that have not fully dried, as cracks can become larger over time.

Different types of woods to use to use for Your Woodworking Project

Another aspect to take into consideration when working on woodworking projects is the type of wood that you must use. Be aware that you aren't limited to plywood. This section will go over the various types of wood that can be used to do woodworking.

Softwood

Softwoods are referred to as that not due to their strength but because they are more fragile than hardwoods, but because they originate from coniferous forests like cedar, pine, and fir. The wood appears to be yellow or reddish. Because coniferous trees tend to grow straight and swiftly they cost less than other kinds of wood. This makes them more sustainable to use.

Below are the kinds of softwood species you can choose from.

The Cedar species is soft and has straight grain. It is a highly fragrant type of wood that is utilized in outdoor woodworking projects, such as furniture and decks for outdoor use because it is able to withstand a variety of moist conditions without getting rotten. The most well-known kind of cedar is western red cedar, which is known for its reddish-colored color.

Fir: Fir usually refers to Douglas fir. This kind of softwood features distinct grain and the color of a reddish brown to it. This kind of wood is employed to make furniture. It doesn't have a distinct grain pattern and therefore doesn't stain well. This is usually used when you intend to paint the furniture. It's inexpensive and is commonly found in a variety of stores for home use.

Pine: Pine is available in various varieties which include sugar, white, and Ponderosa. It is used for creating different kinds of furniture. It is simple to work with, which is why it is also employed by carvers who work with wood. This type of wood can be stained, but you need to seal the wood prior to applying the stain.

Redwood: Redwood is comparable to cedar in its in its resistance to moisture. Redwood is a soft wood and is straight. Also, it has a reddish hue to it. It is very simple to use and quite soft.

Hardwood

Many woodworkers enjoy using hardwood due to their various patterns, textures and shades. Although they are expensive when compared to softwoods, they last longer and give a more exotic look to the woodwork. Below are the various types of hardwoods that you could make use of for woodworking.

Ash: It is distinguished by its white or light straight grains of brown. It is hardness 4. It is a hardness scale from 1-5. Ash wood is a great stain-resistant material but is difficult to come across nowadays. However, you can locate them in huge lumberyards.

Birch The two kinds of birch wood for woodworkers, and they are yellow and white. White birch is similar to the color of maple wood, while yellow birch is characterized by an emerald-colored heartwood with a brownish or yellowish hue. Its hardness is 4 on an overall scale of 5. It is easily available, which means it is less expensive than other kinds of hardwoods. While birch wood is simple to use, it can be difficult to stain because the stain will turn streaky. Paint the wood a better choice.

Cherry: It is popular because it's easy to work with, and it finishes beautifully with oil and stain. Additionally, it develops beautifully over time. The cherry wood is the color of reddish brown for the heartwood, while the sapwood color is white. It's not as tough as birch or ash, and has a softer that is 2 out of five. However, it is employed in the production of exquisite furniture due to the fact that it is grown sustainably in the forest.

Mahogany: The Mahogany variety is prized because of its reddish-brown hue. It also stands out for having a medium-textured straight grain. It has a toughness of 2 out of 5, and it is able to take stain or oil extremely well. While mahogany is an excellent material for working with, it's not cultivated sustainably and can be very costly.

Maple: Maple is available in soft and hard varieties. Both varieties however are more durable than other kinds of woods. It is because the harder maple is a toughness of 5 out of 5, which makes it hard to use. If you're just starting out and want to learn, it is best working using soft maple. It is also less expensive than other hardwoods.

Oak The most popular type of furniture made of wood used by woodworkers. It comes in white and red. This kind of wood is durable and has the toughness rating of four out of five. The white oak is preferred over red oak for furniture, but both are water-resistant, which is why they are able for furniture for outdoor use.

Poplar: It is a hardwood that is affordable, however it is quite soft, with an average hardness of 1. It is distinguished by streaks of green and brown in the heartwood. It is also utilized in making toys, bowls, and small woodworking craft. It isn't considered to be attractive wood, but it does be used using paint, so you can paint over streaks.

Teak: Teak has golden brown hue and has an average hardness at 3 of five. It is extremely resistant to weather conditions, which is why it is used to make outdoor furniture. The issue with teak is that it's becoming harder to find in lumberyards, and they are also quite expensive.

Walnut The hardness of Walnut is rating of 4/5, and it is well-known for its dark brown hue. Walnut wood can be used for accents and as for inlays. While it is a very popular choice, it can be expensive and finding large pieces isn't always easy.

Chapter 11: Toolkits to Utilize

Woodworking is an art that no one can master however, you can take it up as a pastime. As with all crafts it requires a few tools to produce a perfect product within a certain time frame. A professional woodworker must have the tools he needs in accordance with the kind of work they are skilled at. Beginning as a beginner it is essential to have a fundamental knowledge of the tools that you'll use in the near future. Take a look at the list of tools and details on the way each tool works and what it is used for. is used.

Chisel

Chisels are designed to come with an elongated blade as well as the handle. The tool is made from steel to cut or carve the wood. The force can be applied with your fingers or be increased using mallets. The tool is able to be sharpened at any moment it becomes dull. You may require some stones to sharpen your chisel instead of the grinder. It is important to coat them with oils to get the most effective outcomes.

The handle's base is made of metal, and has an elastomer padding to ensure that it can be used without difficulty. Some models have plastic or wood handles, too. The chisel's blades be widened to create any shape of cuts based on the object to be cut. If you plan to keep the tool in use for many years, be sure to maintain the cap on your edge in place and be sure to moisten it periodically or at the end of each use. If you don't have edge caps keep it in a roll , so that the chisels won't slide around in the drawer of the box.

Chisels come in a variety of sizes, and the smaller ones can be used for mortise and abrasion work. When you purchase a chisel be sure to choose one with the handle that is suitable for your hand. Keep a hammer or mallet to help save the head from the chisel.

Another reason to use a chisel is to scrub joints. Anyone who is a beginner can utilize it for a variety of DIY projects.

Claw Hammer

The hammer can be found everywhere. The claw head must be properly balanced against the round head. Since it is a basic tool you should be aware that it's used for driving nails or pulling nails. Hand tools need the power that your muscles. They require proper maintenance. If your claw hammer isn't well-balanced, it could turn in your hands and you could be annoyed.

Its mechanism is quite simple. It is necessary to grasp the handle, and then the head will do the job. The claw hammer on the market has a either a fiberglass or wooden handle. Choose the one you feel at ease. The majority of wooden handles aren't suitable for pulling a lot of nails. However, when you plan to pull a large number of nails, they would be better to use a handle that reduces stress. Also, handles made of steel and fiberglass should be equipped with a rubber grip to ensure comfort and control. A claw hammer of 20 ounces is the most popular type of purchase.

The tape measure

It is an instrument used to determine the precise lengths and to take precise measurements to avoid making mistakes at the end. There are a variety of tape types on the market, ranging from the length of a meters to 10 meters. If you exceed the length the limit, you could face issues such as difficulty moving it.

It's usually in a rubber or metal casing to prevent the possibility of breaking if it falls from the high point. The small size of the item makes it easy to carry around and can be stored in a purse easily. The locking feature allows you to choose the ideal size. If not, the dimensions could differ from 1/8" and can lead to severe problems in the long time.

The hook or tab on the other end of the measuring tape makes it user-friendly. The ruler made of metal inside the tape has a flexible design and is able to roll and unroll with ease.

Screw Drivers

It is essential to have a collection of screwdrivers that are different in your toolkit. They are utilized to drive through screws or nails into various types of types of materials. They can also aid in loosening or secure the parts of wooden or mechanical parts. Phillips, flatheads slots drivers, star drivers are the most common kinds that screw drivers are available. They come in a variety of sizes, and handles are made of plastic, and sometimes covered in metal or rubber.

I'd suggest that you have a long screw driver that has a square-tip to give the maximum torque. A screw driver with a narrow shank is essential to access screws in difficult places. The smaller the shank, more is the force that drives.

A simple trick to drive screws with ease into timber is by applying bee-wax. If bee wax isn't available the soap can be applied on the screws' threads.

The nail was set

Another important hand tool to have before beginning the woodworking process can be nail set. They come in a variety of sizes, and you don't know which one you might require for a specific task. The nail heads are inserted into the wood until they attach to the desired material.

Handsaw

It comes in various designs, however you'll be required to select one based on your requirements. It's function is cutting the wood with its sharp blades, and you need to operate it using hands. A high quality handsaw to finish your woodworking projects shouldn't be neglected. You can cut straight edges, curves or straight edges and create angled cuts dependent on the kind of saw you are using. Blades that are skinny are great for cutting curves , while large blades such as tenon saw cut straight lines. The material used to make the handle could be made of metal, plastic, or wood.

Marking gauge

It assists in marking lines on wood. it functions through adjusting the gauge to the measurement of the line at an edge on the wood. Marking gauges are made from wood and consist of two pieces. A head that can be moved and is able to move upwards and downwards to alter the measurement. It also has the screw made of plastic or metal to secure it. A shaft with a sharp edge to mark the final point.

Marking knife

It is the most basic tool that can be used to create an elegant crease prior to cutting through the wood with the help of a saw. The saw follows the precise line drawn by the sharp edge of the blade and cut the wood fiber precisely.

It's a piece of metal with a handle as well as the blade is thin and sharp on the other end. The handle is made of metal however some prefer wood or plastic handles to improve the quality.

Planer

It's a useful tool to get rid of the excess wood, giving the appearance of the piece to ensure accuracy. It can be useful in thinning wood in order to shape it, and smooth rough patches. Planners are made of metal with a double wooden handle to enhance the effectiveness. A small hole on the bottom of the base is where the blade is located.

Try Square

You'll understand the significance of this hand tool when you step into the world of woodworking. You can test the precision of angles made in wood using the square to test. It is possible to draw straight lines across the wood with it and also determine how straight the wood piece is prior to cutting or cutting.

It comes with a wooden handle and a blade made of metal. The handle is positioned against an object's edge with the metal blade is placed at 90 degrees towards the handle. It is possible to test the squares by this method.

Sandpaper

It's a paper that has abrasives added to it. You can purchase it from markets in various sizes, identified by an identifying number in the reverse.

Sandpaper is employed to make the surface smooth by taking off any excess material or paint. The hand tool can be used in conjunction with a sanding block in order to make a smooth surface.

Mallet

It is similar to the hammer due to their appearance and function closely resemble. They have a larger head when compared to hammers however they are able to avoid damaging objects and can fit it in the right place. The overall impact is similar often.

It is helpful for shaping material since it comes with the head of rubber or wood. It is a secure and practical hand tool.

Clamps

Clamps tighten or fix the material, thereby securing it over the long-term. They function as adhesives by generating an inward pressure. Sometimes, it's used to keep things in place until the adhesive has completely dried.

Pipe clamps bar clamps as well as quick grips comprise varieties of clamps that are employed for woodworking tasks. They are made from metal with some plastic inserts.

Sliding bevel

Sliding bevel is composed of two major components. A blade made of steel and a stock made of wood make it clear. It's primarily used to mark angles of the wood with ease. It comes with a locking function, by which it can be locked at the angle you prefer. It can save you time.

Block Plane

It is essential at the conclusion of your woodworking task. It is a tiny tool which can be cut to make the edges neat and give the woodwork an elegant appearance. The most notable feature of the block plane is that it is equipped with an iron blade set at a lower angle , and it can only be used in one hand, opposed to other planes.

Woodworking tools organization

It is possible that you won't use all the tools you'll need at home, but having them will ensure with the fact that you are able to do any woodworking project at home. The organization of your tools is essential so that you don't need to hunt for them each time they are needed. Also, keeping them in their place of origin can make them more usable for a longer period of time.

Unorganized things lead to the waste of time, and show your individual style. well-organized tools show your professionalism and passion for your work. There is a possibility of having a pegboard to store accessories and tools close to your workspace so you can get them quickly. You can build a beautiful wooden tool box at home for your first attempt at making a project. Tool kits can also be purchased for fasteners. Making sure you have your fasteners and other tools in order can save you a few trips to the hardware store.

Power Tools

Technically speaking, anything that requires electric power to operate is a power tool. Apart from hand tools, there are powerful power tools that simplify your work. It's evident that someone who is new to the field might be concerned about the cost of power tools. But don't worry. I'll give you a seven important power tools that aren't as costly.

Power Drill

It is possible that you will have a cordless drill included in this list, but we're talking about a corded drills that are more powerful and can accomplish much at a lower cost. You'll be thrilled to be able to borrow a tool such as the power drill.

It is available in two sizes.1/2 inches and 3/4 inch. The size is based on the size that the chuck is. A 3/8-inch diameter will meet your needs, however if you want more power and wish to test drilling bigger holes to complete a project, you should choose an inch. You can adjust the speed to suit the speed you prefer while working, but the drill that is cordless has only two speed levels.

Circular Saw

It is a hand-held power tool that can be utilized in many ways. Many people believe that it's not necessary and a table saw could perform the job. It is possible to attach a clamp to the straight edge to get optimal results. It can also be utilized to cut a variety of non-wood products.

If you're planning to buy circular saws, look for one that has more horsepower. In addition, look over the controls for adjustments of the bevel and depth of cut. Make sure that the saw you choose comes with safety features as well as it could pose an issue similar to other cutting tools. Recently, I've come across circular saws powered by batteries on the market. They are light in weight however, they have low horsepower. You can pick one of them based on your preference.

Jigsaw

It's also known it a Sabre Saw. It is an ideal tool for creating curves or circular designs on light materials such as wood or particle boards that have 2 inches of depth. It is recommended for novices since it is relatively easy to change the blades as they start to dull. It is not a bad idea to invest in a high-end jigsaw with adjustable speed and orbital action. It is extremely efficient by reducing the speed when cutting intricately. Someone who is comfortable working with a variable speed jigsaw is not comfortable using a single speed Jigsaw.

Router

A good router to a beginner is the one with a an adjustable base. The plunge router base nowadays is also accessible. What's the difference between them? In the same way, when you use the base router stationary you choose a particular depth and it makes the cut accordingly however, in the plunge router, you can rotate it downwards to cut the desired amount and then remove the router out of stock.

Don't buy one with lower than two HP. Another aspect to keep in mind when buying is that the router should have with a variable speed. The bigger the block, the slower it will be. If you are using an unreliable speed router and you are able to be burning the part. Make sure you have the switch on power within your reach while you are working with the router. Another thing to consider is that the handles need to be easy to hold. The plunge router's handles are on the opposite side that are on the bottom.

A new feature of modern routers is is an integrated electronic feedback system that lets the router sense the load and adjust the speed. It's not cheap however, and is a worthwhile addition.

Compound Miter Saw

Crosscuts made on wood are created using the compound miter saw, which makes the work of woodworkers quite simple. It is helpful in creating beveled, angled or square cuts on the ends of the boards. If you purchase an excellent miter saw, it will come with clearly marked miter gauge. The worker is able to put the saw in lock when they have to mark the angle they require. To cut precise angles the saw may be be angled to at 60 degrees in any direction.

The blade's size in miter saws is 8" 10" 12" as well as 15". The most popular dimension is 10" since 8" isn't big enough, while 12" can be a bit costly. It is a good option if you have the money for it. To make miter saws more efficient, certain manufacturers have included the laser light so that the cut mark is easily discernible.

It can be helpful to the woodworker when he decides cutting two angle in the same piece.

Random Orbital Sander

I would advise every newbie to purchase an orbital sander that is random. The random sanding action will result in an even finish, and the chance that you leave any trace from sanding is reduced. Even though plain sandpaper serves the same purpose and can be purchased for purchase at affordable prices, it's not as effective as the efficiency and time taken by the random orbital sander.

You must consider dust collection filters that are included inside the Sander. It is best if it comes with an air-tight vacuum that can be used to collect dust. The switch in the machine should be sealed to prevent dust from getting into it and making it difficult for it to start and stop. When you purchase, make an effort to turn it off to test the vibrating. You must be confident with it, as certain sanders produce unusual vibrations that cause anxiety for the user.

Table Saw

It is an essential tool that is found in every woodshop. Once you are familiar with the fundamental power tools, you could think about buying the table saw. It is important to look over the features before you purchase it. Make a decision for yourself whether you will need these features in the future projects you are working on or if they're just for the purpose of attracting customers.

It can help you finish large woodworking projects since it's a multi-purpose tool. It can form, groove, square, rip, measure and join. A top quality table saw should have the following characteristics:

A smooth and sturdy working surface

A handle that moves the blade of the saw up and down

Another handle is used to adjust the angles of the blade

A motor with a powerful power that can start by a slight vibrating

The right amount of horsepower to cut the hardwood efficiently.

Modern table saws have large switches that resemble paddles that allows you to turn off or on the device. Blade guards provide protection for woodworkers from the sharp blades of the saw.

I'm sure that after you've read this chapter, you will be aware of the most common tools for woodworking. It will be extremely helpful when working on your projects.

Chapter 12: Tools Of The Traditional Trade

The tools utilized in woodworking can be classified in two categories that are called traditional and Modern. Traditional tools are generally hand-tools that were used in the beginning of woodworking. Chisels, hammers and handsaws are some tools which fall in this category. However, Modern tools are the modern tools are used in the present. The tools that are part of the category of modern tools are Random Orbit Sanders, Circular saw, Jig saw, etc.

In this chapter, we will be discussing the standard tools that an aspiring beginner to woodworking will likely pick.

The Workbench

The use of a quality Workbench is essential for woodworking. This is where the bulk of the work gets done. When selecting a workbench, ensure that you purchase something with an elongated top that is at minimum 3 inches, sturdy support legs that can withstand the wood's weight, with two faces vices. The face vise is designed to ensure that the wood is being worked on stays secure and not scratch the wood.

The Jack Plane

It is a Jack Plane is a multi-purpose bench plane which is employed for smoothing edges and for sizing the timber. It is approximately 15 inches in length and has an edge that is moderately curved. It is referred to as"the Jack Plane because of its relationship to the term "Jack of all trades" which means it's not restricted to just one useful application. The most well-known applications of using the Jack Plane are rough stock removal, board smoothing , and the jointing of edges on boards.

The Block Plane

Block planes are like Jack Planes aesthetically. But, unlike the Jack Plane, Block planes are generally used for trimming end grain, putting Champhers on edges, and joint trimming. If you're looking to purchase the perfect Block plane, make sure you choose models with the rabbet block with a low angle. The low angle rabbet block lets you reduce surfaces directly to other joint joints, or cheeks of tenons. It also will allow you to cut difficult grains easier.

This is the Rip and Crosscut Handsaw

The saw is a crucial tool that is used by woodworkers. It is the primary hand instrument used to cut wood into various dimensions. There are two kinds of saws that are utilized in woodworking, specifically those called the Rip saw as well as the Crosscut saw. The distinction between them is in the way that it is that the blades of the saw are sharpened. It is the Rip tooth of the saw is set so that they go down the grain of wood while cutting.

It is sharpened like an axe. The Crosscut teeth however, are sharpened in a manner similar to the blade edge of an ordinary knife. This is particularly useful when making cuts against the grain wood.

Dovetail Saw

Dovetail saws are the kinds of saw that is used to create Dovetail joins in woodworking. Dovetail joints are a jointery technique that is known by its difficulty in taking it apart. This is due to the tail and pin cuts that are used to join two sides in the timber. The Dovetail saw is equipped with the finest teeth and a ripsaw arrangement for better cutting.

Tenon Saw

It is also known as the Tenon saw is a different kind of saw that is used for cutting tenons in tenon and mortise joineries. The mortise and tenon joint is a common method employed by stonemasons and blacksmiths, which was later modified to wood. It's a form of joinery where a tongue and mortise hole are used in order to connect two boards making it simple and durable.

Mitre Box along with Saw

Mitre box Mitre box can be described as a device that acts as a reference to the Mitre saw to make mitre cuts in a wood board. It is a Mitre box is usually an open-ended box with three sides, which are accessible at the top and both ends, which is where the board can pass through. The box has cut-outs that are angled on the sides which will direct the Mitre saw in cutting certain angles onto the board. The cuts are generally located at 90 degrees or 45 degrees, respectively.

The Coping Saw

A Coping Saw is one of the most commonly used woodworking tools that are available. The Coping Saw has sharp cutting edges and is typically used to cut designs on the boards. The saw and its blades are quite affordable, making it an essential purchase for every woodworker.

Beneveled Edged Chisels for Bench

Chisels are tools with the shape of a knife designed to cut sections of wooden. They are available in a variety of sizes, based on the cutting task being performed. Hand chisels of a smaller size are employed for cutting out fine details on sculptures, while larger chisels can be used to remove large pieces of wood for creating forms. Chisel cutting is usually done manually or using the mallet or hammer in a small size.

Try Square

The Try Square is a tool that is used to measure certain dimensions on a wood board. It is specifically used to determine the precision of right angle measurements of the flat surface of wood. Traditional try squares are made from steel blades which are riveted onto an unfinished wooden piece at 90 degrees. The blades of steel have measurements engraved on them like an ruler.

Sliding T Bevel

Bevel gauge that slides, also known as a bevel gauge is comparable to the try square in terms the measurement of angles made on a wood board. The difference lies in the capacity of the bevel gauge sliding to create and transfer different angles. It is equipped with a metal ruler as well as a handle made of wood that is joined to each other by a thumbscrew which can be adjusted to loosen or tighten. This thumbscrew permits the metal ruler to pivot, and it can be adjusted to a desired angle using an inclinometer or framing square.

Dividers (Compass)

Dividers are actually historic and old-fashioned tools. They are not just used to draw circles, but are also used for transfer of measurements. If you need to measure something and want to duplicate it across it, this is the most effective instrument to use. It is recommended to have two pairs of dividers because you'll typically be moving two measurements at one time.

Marking Gauge

Marking gauges are essential tools for joining tasks. The primary function of a marking gauge is to create the lines in a parallel fashion to an edges or surfaces. The marking gauge consists of three primary parts, which are the beam, the stock and the marking instrument. The stock is moved across the beam and can be tightened with the use of a hand screw. The marking implement is attached at the top of the beam on one side.

Sharpening Tools

Sharpening tools are definitely necessary tools for woodworkers. A lot of woodworking tools come with edges that can be utilized to remove specific pieces. So, keeping these tools sharp is essential. For novices it is recommended you purchase sharpening equipment for your chisels as this is the tool you will use the most often. A grinder that has cool cutting stones and a high-quality water stone, and a honing guide are a few of the most essential sharpening tools that every woodworker should have.

Wooden Mallet

Woodworking is a process of hitting lots of things, so buying a good mallet made of wood is vital. The use of wooden mallets is to make joint joints, to drive nails and strike chisels while cutting joints. It is recommended to use a metal hammer should not be used when hitting a chisel as it can damage the tool. A mallet made from hard wood is the best to purchase since it is very well balanced when held in your hands.

Clamps

Clamps can be very helpful in keeping two wood pieces for joining. They are also able to hold a wood securely while cutting. There are two kinds of clamps that can be used for woodworking, The hand screw clamp as well as the bar clamp. Hand screw clamps are usually used to keep smaller pieces of wood securely as you work on them. The clamps that look like bars however are designed to hold larger pieces of wood to cut rough.

6 inches Combination Square

A 6-inch combination square is usually used to test whether a board is square plank. The squareness of a board is crucial after planning a board to determine its the final dimensions. For someone who is just working on his woodworking skills the combination square 6 inches is among the most effective tools for starting out. There are 12-inch and 16 inch versions that make up the combo square however, for beginners it is the 6 inch that is the best choice.

1/4 " Mortise Chisel

The most popular joinery methods that woodworkers employs is mortise and tenon joint. To accomplish this technique using the mortise chisel of 1/4 inch is required. It's used to create exact mortises (rectangular hole) cut into the wood board into which the tenon is to be placed. Mortise chisels can be purchased for a reasonable price and readily available.

The Folding-rule

The zigzag rule or folding rule is made up of light, thin wooden strips that are riveted at both ends so as to fold. The strips of wood unfold and secure to form a sturdy ruler to take measurements. It comes with measurement marks which are printed or engraving. The folding-rule is commonly employed to create rough length measurements on the board for the purpose of sizing. The folding rule is among the oldest tools that was used in woodworking. It was used to the 1800's.

Chapter 13: Selecting Your Wood

The two main categories of wood are softwood and wood. It is also possible to create plywood-like wood.

The materials you use for a particular job is contingent on many factors, including the strength, durability grain quality, cost stability, weight, strength, color and availability. The majority of woodworkers starting out work using softwood, such as pine. It is soft and easy to use and does not require expensive tools to achieve outstanding results. It's available at local lumberyards and home centers. There are some limitations when it comes to making furniture. The wood is soft, and will be damaged very quickly.

Softwood is derived from an evergreen, or coniferous (cone-bearing) coniferous (cone-bearing) tree. Common ranges are pine spruce and fir, as well as hemlock as well as redwood, cedar and. They are mostly used for construction of homes.

Redwood and cedar are great choices for outdoor projects While pine is typically used in "Early American Country Style" furniture.

Softwoods like pine and a lot of other softwoods will absorb and lose more moisture than hardwoods, which means they are not as sturdy. Purchase the lumber at a minimum of 2 weeks before you begin your project. Keep it in a safe place.

You will discover that softwoods are sold in standard widths and density. For example, a 1X 4 would have a thickness of 1/4" thick , and 3 1/2" wide, which is comparable to construction materials. The product will generally be priced per linear foot, and it will increase for the larger boards.

Hardwood lumber comes of deciduous tree, ones which shed their leaves every year. Most popular domestic varieties include oak and maple, as well as walnut, cherry, birch and poplar. Ash, as well as poplar. Of these common hardwoods, only poplar and red oak are usually available at home centres and in lumberyards. Other hardwoods must be purchased from specialist shops. The products sold at lumberyards and home centers typically are offered in similar dimensions to softwood, and per lineal foot as well.

In specialty stores the density of the hardwood lumber is stated as quarters of an inch. It is that is, when the wood is in rough form. The tiniest piece is 4/4, while the most thick is 16/4. Instead of being smashed into specific measurements, as is the case with the pine species, wood is sold in random lengths and widths.

Handling hardwoods is a bit different than dealing with pine. You cannot use a screw to cut through the wood of a hardwood without making the pilot hole. Planing and cutting hardwoods require the most precise tools.

Hardwoods are great to use in the design of furniture. Ash and oak are often referred by their open grain woods. They are both species that have different parts that are relatively permeable and strong wood. After being stained the open grain parts absorb the color quickly while the harder parts tend to resist. The grain patterns are highlighted and creates a stunning result.

The three species of birch, maple, and cherry are closed-grain hardwoods that exhibit the same texture across the entire board. The poplar wood is also a closed grain wood, but its color ranges from beige to olive-green, and often has purple highlights added to the mix. Due to its unusual coloring the wood is rarely used in furniture pieces that are intended to have a transparent surface. This kind of wood is best painted or stained. Poplar, which is less costly is also a great alternative for framing wood projects.

The durability of hardwood is greater and less prone to damage and scratches. It's also more expensive however, it is likely to last in a higher quality. Softwoods, similar to wood, can be vulnerable to scratches and dents. They also don't have the durability of hardwood. They are also less expensive and are easier to find. Contact your lumber company to demonstrate "Class 1" or "Select Grade" lumber. Be sure that it has dried thoroughly and free of knots and issues. (It may not be perfect but make sure you are aware of the best way to deal with those).

The two most commonly used sheets used in furniture manufacturing include MDF (Medium Density Fiberboard) and Particle Board. Both are made of wood particles, which are then bonded using glue and then bonded with pressure. MDF has smaller particles as compared to Particle Board, so it makes a more smooth and robust product.

MDF performs well and is often used for parts that are molded on painted furniture. Its main disadvantage is that it's heavier than real wood.

Due to their laminated structure that is laminated, they are extremely stable across all sizes. Because the veneers of the panel are usually made sequentially from the same log, the panel should have a consistent appearance and color. The process of matching patterns of sturdy wood to the normally uniform grain pattern of the panels can be a challenge. But, a bit of patience can result in perfect matches in the most visible areas of your job.

Manufactured sheets have limitations. If they are employed regardless of the core edge must be concealed. The surfaces are thin, often less than 1/32 inches. This means that the surface area is susceptible and can split in particular on the rear of a cut. In addition, since the veneer is thin, abrasive sanding could quickly rip through the veneer, exposing the unattractive core beneath.

The type of the type of wood you use will depend on what kind of project you're working on. If the project is going have to paint, you could make use of MVF only. For furniture, it's usually recommended to select items that are likely to be finished well, such as the oak or cedar.

Most likely, you'll get your wood from a lumber supply store or a home improvement shop such as Home Depot or Lowe's. There are some factors to keep in mind when selecting your wood.

In the wood yard, or at the shop there are boards of wood stacked in tall stacks based on length of the board, its quality density, grade wood type and a variety of other categories. In even the stacks that are classified in the same way there are differences in terms of quality, so you should follow these guidelines to select the boards that will fit your woodworking needs.

Don't take boards that you don't like! For beginners in the lumberyard, it may seem like they must go with the boards initially provided to them. Be sure to look over every board with care and send them back in the event that they don't meet your expectations. Why would you spend money on a damaged board that is not going to be able to work for your project? Removing boards isn't an insult, but an opportunity to purchase the wood you will need and get into the habit before you get into.

Check for straightness. The board should be held at an eye level at one end and the other placed on the ground. Examine the board's surface to determine if it is covered with apparent twists or curves. Certain projects can work with an angled board, However, for beginners working with curved boards, it may be too complicated.

Find warping and splits. Take a look at every side to check whether there are long splits or edges that are deformed. Splits and warps decrease the amount of wood you could use to build your project, therefore avoid boards that could result in a lot of wasted wood.

Knotholes can be attractive in certain types of woodworking projects. So If you're trying to find the most knotty piece wood, it's okay. If not, check your boards for knots which could turn out to be waste wood or knots that could fall off and cause holes or weak spots within your cut pieces. For woodworking projects that are great or projects that require a straightand even grain, quarter-sawn lumber is a great choice for the same wood graining but it's more expensive than regular plain-sawn lumber. Select whether you would like to purchase the straight grain prior to choosing the boards.

Examine each board to determine if the hue is sufficient to suit your needs and ensure that there's not a large number of wormholes or damaged components. Also, look for chalk marks or pen markings , or marks that aren't likely to be removed quickly.

Older boards that were salvaged from barns, or from other projects can be intriguing and fun to work with. But, before buying or acquiring salvaged lumber, be sure to look for signs of decay. If the wood is spongy or soft or is showing signs of fungi It may not hold up as well as project wood.

Chemically treated lumber and pressure-treated lumber can be used for outside projects. They are more able to withstand temperature and wetness changes. If you're planning to build an outside deck or outdoor project, make sure you request treated lumber. If not, untreated lumber is the better choice.

A beginner woodworker should start with soft woods, such as pine or spruce. They are less difficult to use, and eventually, you'll be able to advance to more challenging woods such as cedar and oak. You're almost ready to begin but before that we'll look at some security guidelines that the best woodworkers adhere to.

Chapter 14: Benches, Chairs, and Stools (Intermediate Plan)

1. Work Bench

If you're serious about your woodworking then you must have solid work benches. Here's a bench can be built in less than a single day.

Materials:

2x2s to frame the frame and legs

2 x4 wood for the frame

1/4" plywood that can be used as a top for a workbench

Circular saw

Bar clamps

Chisel

Square

Hand drill

Screws

Wood glue

Steps:

Step 1: Cut off the legs. The length must be 78 centimeters. Make use of a measuring tape as well as pencil for marking the wooden.

STEP 2: Next you'll need to cut the pieces that join the legs. Cut four 2x4 pieces that are about 55 centimeters in length. After that, you can assemble the frame by nailing and screwing the pieces to each other.

Step 3: Next you should drill holes on the edges of the frame. Attach the legs. After that, screw them in the holes you've already drill.

Step 4: Next you can screw the rails onto the legs. It's simpler to do this when the bench is lying on its back.

Step 5 5. Cut the wood to size to the frame. Next, attach to the back of the bench onto the bottom.

Done! This workstation only costs around $15! Imagine all the money you'll save when you build an item of furniture from scratch.

2. Three-Legged Stool

Materials:

Pine log

Screws

Power Sander or Sand Paper

Varnish

Band saw

Planer

Three aspen logs

Knife

3 aspen logs

Hammer

Nails

Steps:

Step 1: Cut a part of the timber out of the log with the chainsaw

Step 2: Cut the wood to about 2 inches thick.

Step 3: Mark an outline of a circle on the wood, then cut the circle with a band saw.

STEP 4: After that flatten the surface using a plane. Cut three 14 inch aspen logs. These will be the legs for your stool.

STEP 5: Remove the aspen logs with the knife. Then the sanding process begins.

Step 6 Step 6: Nail the legs onto a the log of pine using the Hammer. Then paint the stool with varnish. Then, let it dry.

Now, you've got an stools! You can build any number of stools you want.

3. Simple Chair

This is a basic 2-x4 chair design which you can put into place within just a few hours.

Dimensions

17 1/2 " 18 1/2"x 37 1/4 "

Materials:

2 pieces of 2x4s that are 10 feet long

One piece, 8 foot long of 2x4

Drill

Saw

2 1/2 " screws

4" screws

Wood filler

Wood glue

Paint

Sander

Cut List

A two pieces 37 1/4 to make back legs

B . - Four pieces of 10-1/2 " for front and back boards

C Two pieces 16 1/2" as front legs

D two pieces out of 15" side boards

E - 1 piece 13 1/2 "

F Three pieces in 18 1/2 " to make the seat

G Two pieces from 17" in length for seat sides

Steps:

Step 1: Make the back.

First, you need to construct your chair's back. It is necessary to take the two legs at the back and three boards for the front and back. Assemble them using the diagram below. Attach the back and front pieces to each other with two 1/2-inch pocket screws as well as a Kreg Jig. It is also possible to make use of wood glue.

Step 2: assemble the front.

When you've built the back piece, you'll need to build the front by assembling the front legs and back piece as seen in the image below:

Step 3: Put together the chair.

Utilize the sideboard pieces to join the front and back parts. Connect these pieces to the back and front parts of the chair with an screw gun. Take the following illustration to guide you:

Step 4: Include the help.

Install 13 1/2 "long in the back of the opening to the seat. This gives the seat boards a bit of room to sit.

STEP 5: Put in the seat.

Join the seat with screws and wood glue. Follow the steps below.

Step 6: Get it done.

Sand the chair before you apply paint.

Woodworking Projects for KITCHEN (ADVANCE Plan)

1. Storage under the sink:

To expand the storage area in you kitchen area, the ideal method is to create an the under-sink storage system. There are many cabinets that are not utilized due to their inaccessibility. The under-sink cabinet is typically overlooked because you must be kneeling down with the aid of a torch in order to look for things in the cabinet. We are offering you a how to make an easy-to-pull out drawer that can hold lots of items, and provide being accessible.

The first step is to must determine the area that you wish to use for the drawers. It could be a single drawer , or multiple drawers based on the area and the requirements. They are also able to slide them over edges of pipes.

Materials:

2-ft. 2 feet. Of 1/2"-inch Plywood

Half-sheet of 3/4-inch hardwood plywood

Two linear feet. made of one-inch by 6 inches of maple

Linear Ft. of 1 in. 4 inches Maple

1-5/8-inch screws

Four 20-inch ball bearing slides

Wood glue

Drill

Measuring tape

Saw

Things to write about

Sand paper

How to Use The Space Drawers:

Take measurements of the space you'd like to build the drawers.

Create a base using the wood, which is one-quarter inch large (for an A).

Make the drawer one inch smaller than the indentation that is between the partitions

Take out all drawer components.

Sand them with sandpaper and apply two coats finishing material.

Place the drawer slides on 3/8-inches of spacer, level to the front edge that forms an intonation (B).

Connect them in the indentation, then fix them using screws.

Place the other drawers in the same way using a 3/4 inch spacer to make an appropriate space and secure them by using screws that are attached to the sides of the tray, which is level with the front.

Then, attach your base onto the lower part of the cabinet and fix it using the help of screws.

You can now slide the drawers into the cabinet.

Steps to make the Side Drawers work:

To construct this side drawer it is necessary to follow these steps

In the beginning, you have to create the cleats (K) to help support of side drawers. Additionally, they must be line with one another. Be sure to measure them accurately in order to be able to take them out to take them out, they will not be stuck because of hinges on the doors of the cabinet.

Attach all the pieces of the drawer using the aid of screws as well as wood glue.

The slides must be secured to the sides using the aid of glue and screws. Be sure that they are securely connected.

After you have completed all the work, remove the edges of the wood using the aid of the sandpaper.

Final Assembly:

The first step is to must build an initial base to support the bottom drawers. of the drawers on the bottom.

The base is erected on the lower part of the cabinet, just in front of the hinges on the door of the cabinet.

It is necessary take a cut wood to the dimensions of the cabinet's bottom and then fix it by using a screw that is placed behind the hinges.

A base's front edges must be aligned with the frame.

The slides are now attached to the sides of the drawers to the sides.

Create a 3 1/2 inch template for the cleat as well as on the longer side of every piece of wood.

Draw a sketch of the template

Create holes around these marking lines using the aid of a drill

Then, attach the cleats to the sides of the cabinet using the aid of screws. To temporarily secure this cleat, you can make use of an edging piece of plywood.

Put all the drawers in their respective places. The storage under the sink is set.

2. Pot rack for hanging

The hanging pot rack is a necessity of every kitchen and can be found in every house. The main benefit they offer is that they can accommodate many pots within a small space.

Racks for hanging pots can be made at home, with the aid of materials that are readily available and very simple techniques that require lesser time and effort.

Materials:

Hardwood

Bar clamps

Saw

Sandpaper

Steel wool

Measuring tape

Square

Paintbrushes

Metal file

1 1/2" brad nails

Four screw hooks

S-hooks

3/8-inch wooden furniture button

Wood glue

135 15-foot chain

1-5/8" screws 1-5/8"

Two screw hooks

1x2x6' of board

Polyurethane

1x3x6' boards

Stain

1x2x4' of board

Copper pipe

Wood filler

18 x 1 1/4-inch wire brads

Steps:

In the beginning, you'll have to cut the wood to the desired lengths , as indicated above using the any wood you like.

Cut the ends of the wire made of copper following cutting

Clean the pipe using a bit of steel wool. Make sure you rub in a single direction across every inch of pipe. This will add luster on the pipes.

Making rails:

Utilizing the first image, cut out the rails on the sides.

Utilizing the second picture, create the drill hole into the rails in order to hold them in the middle.

Begin attaching the rail to the support at the lowest point with the bottom edge, in line with the angle cut by placing its centre on the other end of the rail.

Join the rails by the aid of screws and wire brads

Repeat this process to complete the second half of the bundle.

Then, you can begin putting the other rails of support at the same level with the lower edge. Make them stronger by using wire brads and glue.

Assembling the base:

Start putting the end rails so that they are aligned position with the top edge of one side rail, and the opposite towards the end of the supporting rail that are attached on the other side rail. They should be level to ensure you can see the supporting rail located at the lower end.

Make the hole in the shape of 3/8 inch . Attach 3/8 from the furniture button to it. Then, strengthen them with the screws as well as glue.

Make sure to cut the wire to the dimension listed above.

Then, place the copper wire in the holes that are made in the rails supporting it. To allow it to pass through them, apply liquid soap or wax on them.

The remaining two sides of the track are joined in a level of support for the rail against the rails on the sides and copper pipe.

Create countersunk holes with the aid of a drill of 3/8 inch in size. Fix them using the aid of screws and glue.

Then apply glue to furniture buttons where they're connected and place them in the screw holes on the side rails.

Then fill in any hole caused by the nail, sand or stain.

Apply polyurethane

Make four holes for screw eyes, which are 3 1/2 inches from the end of side rails.

Next, drive the screw eyes until all the threads have been completely inserted into

Its hanging rack is in place

Hanging Up:

They can be hung on the joist based on the position of the screw eyes as well as the length of the Joist.

Chapter 15: Woodworking Projects

PROJECT 1. MAKING A Wooden Chopping Board

The materials required are:

* Tasmanian Oak (1 x 3.0m x 42mm 19mm)

* Meranti (1 x 2.7m x 42mm x 19mm)

* Aquadhere External Adhesive (1 500ml)

* Small Paint Brush

* A bucket of water and an old Newspaper Rag

Small bits of wood

TOOLS REQUIRED:

* 2 Clamps 250mm opening capacity

* Carpenters square

* Cork block for sanding

* Hand saw

* Sanding block-course, Fine and medium sandpaper

* Hand plane

* Additional tools: Router, Belt Sander, Jig Saw

PROCESS

Decide the length and width of the desired chopping surface and this one is 400mm (L) 250mm (W).

Dividing the width in 19 which is the width of the lumber (250/19 equals 13.15). For the same color of timber on both sides, you'll require an odd number of parts (13 pieces).

* Select the color of lumber you'd like to have to use for the edges on the outside (7 white colored or dark).

Cut your pieces to length , and then lay them on the ground (42mm length side up) in an alternating pattern of colors.

Apply the water-based adhesive to all the pieces other than the final one, then spread it by using the help of a brush to ensure total coverage.

* Set the entire piece on the edge with a edge that is covered in glue to form a row on the side of the wood.

* Then, you bring all pieces together , even the last one which you didn't put glue on.

* Using a carpenter's square make sure the ends are straight, but you could also use your eyes.

Apply clamps with a few scrap pieces to prevent the clamps from forming edges. Be sure to press down to make sure the pieces are level prior to tightening them for the final time.

With clamps on and the board leveled , flip it and pull out the paper bucking that could be stuck to the side to the back of the board.

Finally, use a damp rag to clean off any glue that has squirted onto every side. Once you've removed all glue , wipe it off using a dry rag to take off any excess water.

Project 2: MAKING A MIRROR FRAME

Material and tools:

* A piece of Birch plywood.

* Chair rails that have an apron cut into the back.

* Molding.

* Glue.

* Screws made of wood.

* Circular saw.

• Nail guns and nail.

* Mirror.

Paintbrushes, paint and brushes.

* Wire chain.

PROCESS

Select a piece of wood you'd like to utilize to build your frame. Oak is a good choice for an area that is dark or pine, which can help to make the room appear more light. If you're looking for lighting in your space, then you could use redwood, cherry or mahogany. These are more dark-colored woods. You can also use birch plywood to reduce costs.

* Take the mirror you're making the frame for, and place it onto the wooden (birch plywood) then mark the measurements it's got across the plywood's center.

Take the mirror off and cut out the measurements you have marked.

* Cut an armrest that will allow the notch to fit well within the plywood's opening. Attach the rail onto the frame's boarder that is inside. Make sure that the notch on the rail is located inside the edge . This helps to prevent the mirror from falling out of the frame's front.

* Take the big molding and cut it to create it to go around the exterior of the mirror frame . put it down with glue and nail it into the frame.

The frame should be painted.

Attach a board to the back of the frame with the use of screws to secure the mirror.

* Finally on the back each facet of the frame place a long metal chain which will help in hanging the mirror. Be sure that the chain is sturdy enough to provide additional support.

3. MAKING A BAR STOOL

Materials and Tools

* 4 pieces of lumber to make legs for stools (3 inches of thickness) They should be circular or squared, and cut to the desired length

* Drill

* Wood glue

* 1 circular or square seat, approximately 4 inches thick

* Chisel

* 4 large screws (3 inches long)

• Varnish, stain or color

* Upholstery and padding

PROCESS

* Decide on the dimensions of your stool based on the bar's height, and then decide whether you'd like your seat to be square or circular.

* Choose the type of wood that you want to employ e.g. beech, maple, oak. Be sure the seat is approximately 4 inches thick and two feet wide. The edges should be sanded and then cut using a handsaw in the event you need to change or improve the look of the design.

* Cut holes into each of four corner of chair of the bar stool. Make use of the chisel for digging into the hole to a certain extent, and then make it big enough to accommodate a screw head. Then, you can insert screws into the four corners on the bottom of the bar stool's seat. The sharp end of the screw must be extending just enough into the hole, so that you are able to secure the legs of the stool from each of them.

• Trim the legs of the wooden stools to the height of the stool you prefer. Make sure that you have at minimum 3 inches in thickness to ensure security. Sand the bottoms and tops of the pieces to create rounded edges.

• Place the legs of the bar stool. Utilize the drill to create an opening halfway through at the foot's top. This is where you'll place the sharp ends of the screws into the seat of the bar stool. This basically means joining the pieces.

* Squeeze a few drops of glue onto the seat holes and screw heads. Then, carefully insert the newly emerged screw into the hole on top of the leg. Screw them until you feel a little resistance in the snugness of the fit between the seat of the bar stool along with the legs.

* Clean up any wood glue that is left. The bar stool should be raised and allow it dry. Make sure that the bar stool is sturdy on all four feet without moving.

PROJECT 4: THE PROCESS of constructing a wine rack

These are the basic steps typically required when building an easy wine rack of wood.

* Copy the design you've chosen to a precise drawing which will be used as a guideline for cutting the pieces.

Cut the wood starting with the end panels and then the cross rails. The cross rails serve as a container for the bottles.

* Drill the holes into the wood. If you're using screws to help hold the rack in place, drilling the holes for screws will prevent the wood from splitting.

* Next, you create the frame. Some wine racks depend on notches that are cut into the ends of the panels as well as cross rails to secure the elements supporting them. Some will use screws to fix the pieces. Connectors must be secure to ensure safety and stability.

* Remove the wine bottle support. Many arches, shelves or partial circles or round holes, you can place bottles individually. If the rack does not support the bottle with the neck alone, make use of a drill press or hole saw to create two different sizes of holesan arch smaller to support the neck and one larger arch to support the bottom of the bottle. The saws should be slightly bigger that the size of the base as well as the neck of the bottle.

Sand until smooth, and then apply the desired finish. If the rack features a top that is going to serve as a serving surface and serving, polyurethane is a good choice to keep the surface safe. In the event that you're using Tung oil or antique oil, coat it without restriction. Allow it to sit for a few minutes before wiping off any excess. It should dry before going through the process again.

PROJECT 5 PROCESS OF MAKING A GARDEN BENCH

Materials and Tools

5. Five pieces wood (2 4x8 feet)

One piece wood (1 4 x 4 feet)

*1 piece wood (4 4x4x8 feet)

Two threaded rod (3/8-in.-dia 36-in.)

* 4 nuts for each hex as well as washers (3/8-in.). The diameter outside is 9/16 inch.

* Polyurethane glue

* 1 wooden dowel (1-in.-dia.)

* 1 box decking screws (1 5/8-in.)

* 1 box galvanized finish nail (1 1/2-in. (4d))

PROCESS

* Use a circular or power mister saw as well as the crosscut guide, then cut four feet, twelve spacers, to length, and 9 seats boards. Utilize a table saw for cutting the tenon off one leg's upper part. Make shoulder cuts in the opposite side of every leg. fix a stop block that is small to cut fence. The outside blade should at least 3 1/2" away from the block. Adjust the blade to be 1 3/8 inches tall, place the leg on the stop block . Use an miter gauge and push it along the blade.

* Flip the legs and to make a shoulder cut. As you hold the leg in place against the miter gauge, move the fence away from the front and make several passes across the blade in order to take away the the

bulk of each tenon. Make the paring perfect with using an incredibly sharp chisel.

Nail up to six 2x4 seat boards 3 1/2 inches in size as well as 3/4" thick for spacers. With the help of 1 1/2 inch galvanized nail for finishing and polyurethane glue fix the block to the the outer edge of 3 1/2 inches to the other end.

* To secure one leg to each end of two seats which don't have spacers utilize glue as well as 1 5/8-inch galvanized decking screw. On the two outer seats boards, for counter bored holes , mark the central locations for the rods and nuts that keep your seat in place. Then, make a 3/4-inch hole using a spade bit with a diameter of 1 inch. This plug of wood will get received through the holes counter bored, and will conceal the hex nuts at the rods' ends which are threaded.

Create a plywood jig and attach it to an appropriate drill guide to to drill the 7/16-

inch diameter holes for rods. This will ensure that the hole you drill through each piece is precisely placed relative to the board's edge. Make sure to set the jig so that it is at the top of each seat before drilling into the spacer block and board.

* Use a workbench and secure all the pieces together. Then, Hacksaw every threaded rod until they reach a length of 19 inches. To the rod's end thread a nut, take off the nut and remove any damage caused by the saw. Use hammer strikes that are light to push each rod through the hole.

* Insert an nut and washer on the ends of each rod and then using a 9/16-inch socket, to tighten it.

* Inside each hole, glue a dowel and cut it to be flush with the surface of your chair board.

* Use either 80 or 100-grit sandpapers for smooth surfaces. Then use an unclean brush to get rid of any dust that has been

sanded. Use a transparent wood preserver to ensure adequate protection for the wood. Clean off fallen leaves which could stain the bench and keep the bench inside during winter.

PROJECT 6. MAKING A WOODEN BOOKSHELF

MATERIALS

* Tape Measure

*Wood

* Sandpaper

Sheet of blank paper

*Pencil

* Wood

* Table saw (optional)

* Safety Glasses

* Power Screwdriver

* Screws

* Glue

* Safety Gloves

PROJECT PREPARATION

Pick the place you would like to place the bookshelf . Then determine what your desired the width, height and depth to be. Tape to confirm that the measurements are for the entire area as well as the bookshelf, and then write these measurements down.

Create a sketch of what you want your bookshelf to appear and indicate the amount of shelves you would like to have within the unit. Think about the type of book and how many things you'll put on the bookshelf you've created. This will allow you to determine whether you'll require a larger wood to provide more assistance or not.

Create an inventory of how much wood you'll require and the size needed. Take measurements of width, height, and depth measurements you have taken to determine the dimensions of each piece you will need. Remember that you must purchase piece of wood that is similar in type and thickness. For instance, if you want building a traditional bookshelf, you'll require two sides that are the width and height you want one top and one bottom piece with the dimensions and width you want, a back piece, and the number of shelves that you would like to have. If your pieces are large and thick, you'll need to take into account the thickness of your piece by making the pieces to fit your preferred dimensions: width + height + thickness.

* Select the type of wood that you prefer, ensuring you are sure that it's durable and has no visible imperfections.

Wear a safety glass and then use a tablesaw to cut the wood to the desired size, if you did not cut them into the proper size at the wood yard. Take note that this process is best done at your own expense if have previous experience cutting wood with the table saw.

* Smooth the wood's edges with a piece of sandpaper.

* Use a pencil mark small lines on the sides of one of the pieces. This will tell exactly where you would like each shelf to rest.

PROCESS

* Grab the piece of side which you created the small drawn lines using the pencil and place it on the floor , while it is raised to its right side. Repeat the same process with the shelves, but make sure to place it in line with the side piece on which you first made your pencil marks to be used to determine the best place for shelves.

Apply a little wood glue on the surface in which the two pieces will join. Make use of a screwdriver to secure the two pieces together starting from the outside side from the piece that is facing outwards to the middle of the shelves thickness. Repeat the process three times, and ensure that it is evenly spaced out based on the size of your piece. The screws' sizes you'll need will depend upon the size of the wood you choose. When the thickness of the piece of wood is multiplied by 2 , it is the same as what the size of screw.

Repeat Step 1, 2 and 3 until you've connected all these shelves on the top side piece. Make sure to make sure that each shelf is aligned with the pencil placement marks you created earlier.

* With the wood glue as well as a screwdriver, join the top and bottom pieces in the same way you attached each shelf. Be sure that the top and bottom pieces are aligned equally with the bottom or the top part of your sidepiece in order to prevent shifting.

* Take the second of the piece, and set it sitting up on its own side, just like the rest of the pieces. It should be aligned equally with the top and bottom pieces of the bookshelf on the open side. With the help of wood glue, and using a screwdriver with

a power tool similarly to the previous steps , you can join the second side piece to the top and bottom pieces as well as to the shelves. Be sure that the shelves are straight and level prior to you attach screws.

The back piece should be placed on top of the bookshelf skeleton you've just made. Place the back piece in a uniform manner with all the corners of your bookshelf being sure that the bottom is level so that it doesn't tilt. Make use of the power screwdriver fix the back piece to every corner of the bookshelf as well as other evenly spaced locations all around the bookshelf.

• Stand your bookcase up, then place it on its new location and smooth out any rough edges using sandpaper.

Conclusion

Woodworking is a process and is not a destination. It is important to take your time and spend as much time as you can in order to make amazing projects you will enjoy along with other people. Doing a rush on your first project could result in disappointing and poorly finished projects that could reduce your desire to return to woodworking in the future. If the outcomes are excellent then you'll be eager to tackle another project . This is the way you will get to learn more tips and methods for amazing projects in the near future.

The key to successful woodworking is having fun. Consider it a hobby and enjoy it. Make a list of projects you would like to tackle and create a plan for the project, and then begin working with it as soon as feasible. Be sure to enjoy every step and observe the amazing results that are. When there's excitement the results will always be fantastic and the success comes at the end.

Many people's biggest fear is starting. If you're passionate for woodworking, then take it on. Don't hesitate to gather every tool for woodworking you are familiar with; simply pick a few of them and begin with a fun but simple project. When it is completed you'll be prepared to tackle the next project. Along along the way, you'll have a few additional tools. When you get the fifth task you'll have all the tools that you will need for your project.

www.ingramcontent.com/pod-product-compliance
Lightning Source LLC
Chambersburg PA
CBHW071839080526
44589CB00012B/1057

9781748529 58